Composing for Silent Film

Composing for Silent Film offers insight, information, and techniques for contemporary composition, arrangement, and live score performance for period silent film. A specialized music composition guide, this book complements existing film scoring and contemporary music composition texts. This book helps today's composers better understand and correctly interpret period silent film, and to create and perform *live scores* that align with films' original intentions, so that audiences notice and grasp fine points of the original film.

Composing for Silent Film analyzes period silent film and its conventions – from Delsarte acting gestures to period fascinations and subtexts. As a practical composition text, it weighs varying approaches, including improvisation, through-scoring, "mickey-mousing," handling dialogue, and dividing roles amongst players. It steers composers towards informed understanding of silent film, and encourages them to deploy contemporary styles and techniques in exciting ways.

For clarity and concision, examples are limited to nine canonical silents: *Metropolis*, *Dr. Jekyll and Mr. Hyde*, *The Mark of Zorro*, *Sunrise: A Song of Two Humans*, *The Black Pirate*, *Nosferatu*, *The Phantom Carriage*, *Daisy Doodad's Dial*, and *The Golem*.

Jack Curtis Dubowsky is a composer, author, music editor, educator, and filmmaker. Books include *Intersecting Film, Music, and Queerness* and *Easy Listening and Film Scoring 1948–78* (Routledge 2021). Dubowsky is a member of the Academy of Television Arts and Sciences, the Recording Academy, the Motion Picture Editors Guild, and a fellow of the Virginia Center for the Creative Arts.

Composing for Silent Film

Jack Curtis Dubowsky

LONDON AND NEW YORK

First published 2024
by Routledge
4 Park Square, Milton Park, Abingdon, Oxon OX14 4RN

and by Routledge
605 Third Avenue, New York, NY 10158

Routledge is an imprint of the Taylor & Francis Group, an informa business

© 2024 Jack Curtis Dubowsky

The right of Jack Curtis Dubowsky to be identified as author of this work has been asserted in accordance with sections 77 and 78 of the Copyright, Designs and Patents Act 1988.

All rights reserved. No part of this book may be reprinted or reproduced or utilised in any form or by any electronic, mechanical, or other means, now known or hereafter invented, including photocopying and recording, or in any information storage or retrieval system, without permission in writing from the publishers.

Trademark notice: Product or corporate names may be trademarks or registered trademarks, and are used only for identification and explanation without intent to infringe.

British Library Cataloguing-in-Publication Data
A catalogue record for this book is available from the British Library

Library of Congress Cataloging-in-Publication Data
Names: Dubowsky, Jack Curtis, author.
Title: Composing for silent film / Jack Curtis Dubowsky.
Description: [1.] | Abingdon, Oxon; New York: Routledge, 2024. | Includes bibliographical references. |
Identifiers: LCCN 2023059336 (print) | LCCN 2023059337 (ebook) | ISBN 9781032184210 (hardback) | ISBN 9781032184227 (paperback) | ISBN 9781003254447 (ebook)
Subjects: LCSH: Silent films–Musical accompaniment. | Silent film music–Instruction and study.
Classification: LCC MT64.M65 D83 2024 (print) | LCC MT64.M65 (ebook) | DDC 781.5/42–dc23/eng/20231222
LC record available at https://lccn.loc.gov/2023059336
LC ebook record available at https://lccn.loc.gov/2023059337

ISBN: 9781032184210 (hbk)
ISBN: 9781032184227 (pbk)
ISBN: 9781003254447 (ebk)

DOI: 10.4324/9781003254447

Typeset in Times New Roman
by Deanta Global Publishing Services, Chennai, India

Contents

Acknowledgments	*ix*
Preface	*xi*

1 Silent film conventions   1
   Story, storytelling, plot, narrative, and themes 1
   Issues and cultural contexts of the silent period 3
   Mechanical conventions 4
      Reels 4
      Establishing shots 4
      Close-up 4
      The close-up as a cliché 5
      Intertitles 6
   Cultural fascinations and conventions 8
      Science and medicine 8
      Psychology 10
      Influenza and disease 10
      Warfare and military technology 10
      Racism and colonialism 12
      Programming suitability 13
      Misogyny and gender roles 14
      Queerness 15
   Acting style 15
      Delsarte 16
      Dalcroze 24
      Controlled acting 26
      Comedy 30
      Acting and your original musical score 31
   Special effects 32

      Editing conventions 34
          Bridging transitions 35
          Music's role in continuity 36
          Editing tricks 38
          Lost and damaged footage 38
      Notes 39
      Bibliography 41

2 Consider your film   44
      Formalist reading 45
          Film funning 45
      Apparatus theory 46
      Studying cultural context 47
      Who needs to prepare, and how much preparation is needed 48
      Watching in silence 49
      Repetitive viewing 49
          Subplots 50
          Character identities 50
          Character arcs 50
          Locations 51
          Background sounds 51
          Environmental sounds 52
          Offscreen sounds 53
      Spotting: choosing which moments to play 54
          Cue lists, cue sheets, and spotting notes 55
          Scene divisions 57
      Tentpoles: important sequences 59
      Budgeting and rights 59
      Notes 61
      Bibliography 62

3 Consider your score   63
      Plan your themes 63
      Sketch your themes 64
      Choice of ensemble 66
          Instrument characteristics and combinations 66
          Solo piano 68

Theater organ 69
The electronic musician 70
Duet 71
Small ensemble 71
Midsize ensemble 72
Orchestra 73
Dividing duties among players 74
Exploiting or avoiding clichés 75
Timing: leading, coinciding, or following 76
Environmental effects 77
Emotional readings 78
Hallucinations and dream sequences 79
Comedy 80
Chases 81
The end 82
Notes 82
Bibliography 83

4 Communicate your score   84
Compositional style, tonal language, musical approaches 84
Avant-garde 84
Pastiche 85
Responsiveness and mickey-mousing 86
Improvisation 88
Structured improvisation 88
Motivic improvisation 89
Coaching improvisation 91
Notation techniques 92
Fully notated score with extracted parts 92
Lead sheet 93
Short score 95
Box notation 96
Text instructions 96
Word score 97
Themes and cue book 98
Conductor hand symbols 104
Combinations 106

Conducting techniques and issues 107
    Sight lines and visibility 107
    Clarity 110
    Cueing entrances and exits 110
    Helping balances 111
    Tempos and dynamics 111
Equipment 112
A conclusion 113
Notes 114
Bibliography 115

Glossary   *117*

Acknowledgments

Above all, I want to thank musicians past and present of the Jack Curtis Dubowsky Ensemble from whom I have learned so much and with whom I have experimented and road-tested different approaches, methods, and ideas. They have suffered through starvation wages, delayed checks, conducting fails, missing courtesy accidentals, cramped rehearsal spaces, long drives, candid photography, and social media posts. These musicians include, at one time or another:

Michael G. Bauer
Marc T. Bolin
Joshua Britt
Ellen Burr
Alicia Byer
Paul Curtis
Nicholas Deyoe
R. Scott Dibble
Trevor Dolce
Stevie Garcia
Hall N. Goff
Jonathan Grasse
John Graves
Audrey Harrer
Zoe Hartenbaum
Erika Johnson
Rebecca Lynn
Angelo Metz
Fred Morgan
Gabriel SLAM Nobles
Laura Osborn
Kevin Schlossman
Jeff L. Schwartz
Charles Sharp

Sean Sonderegger
Sean Stackpoole
Henry Webster
Scott Worthington
Lisa Yoshida

It is from your musicians that you will learn the most. It is not always in the form of an answer to a question, nor is it always the knowledge you sought.

I would like to thank people I've worked with: bookers, theater managers, press people, publicists, writers, reviewers, photographers, volunteers, and projectionists. These include Bret Berg, Logan Crow, Jan van Dijs, Craig Hammill, Kerstin Kansteiner, and Kurt Nishimura, who have all helped me tremendously.

I'd like to thank academic colleagues for their help, especially J. Anthony Allen, Annette Davison, Colin Roust, Charles Sharp, and my own *Music for Media Ensemble* students. My editor Heidi Bishop deserves great thanks for her patience, interest in my fanciful book proposals, and putting up with me in general.

I'd like to thank all the people who came to see our shows. I learned what resonates with an audience, what works, and what doesn't. They taught me how timing is essential, a theme that runs through this book.

Preface

Composing for Silent Film is a specialized music composition guide that offers insight, information, and techniques for contemporary composition, arrangement, and performance of *live scores* for period silent film.

Composing for Silent Film helps composers better understand and correctly interpret period silent films, and to create and perform live scores that align with films' original intentions, so that audiences notice and grasp fine points of the original film.

This book is *not* about restoring, reconstructing, or imitating period film scores – important work, but outside the purview of this composition book. Nor is this book about *film funning*, a historical and contemporary practice where music offers its own wry, witty, or comedic commentary on a film.

Rather, this book encourages today's composers to use their own voice and contemporary techniques to create scores that are faithful to silent film.

Objectives

This book is an **analysis of period silent film and its conventions** – from Delsarte acting gestures to period fascinations and subtexts – and a **practical composition text**, weighing varying approaches and concerns, including improvisation, through-scoring, *mickey-mousing*, handling dialogue, notation, and dividing roles amongst players.

Interest in *new*, original, live music for silent film has surged. Composers and ensembles – student and professional – enjoy the challenges and creative opportunities, but navigate these films awkwardly when they:

- misunderstand the vocabulary and conventions of silent film;
- "jam" over or under-rehearse the film;
- poorly imitate perceived silent film music conventions;
- misinterpret messages and major themes.

This book intends not to curtail musicians' ideas or creativity, but to steer them toward an informed understanding of silent film, and to encourage them to deploy contemporary styles and techniques in exciting ways.

Why this book?

Perhaps you have seen live score events where the ensemble did not *fully appreciate or understand* the film, or used it as a backdrop to do their own thing: an extended jam of some sort, meandering noodling, or bloviated orchestral adventures. Maybe this music made the film seem long, boring, or old, too.

As a composer, performer, and conductor of live scores, I wrote this book to encourage musical freedom, as well as synchronicity of music and image. I want live scores to assist details, nuance, and subplot that might otherwise pass unnoticed. I want film to pop with vibrance, intensity, and meaning. My formal training is in music composition. I've written two previous books on film music. I've worked professionally in Hollywood films and television. My approach combines scholarship and practice, with a particular goal in mind.

This book takes the opinionated approach that our *goal* is to *create scores that support silent film*, rather than undermine, mock, or exploit it as a vehicle for facile self-aggrandizement. There *is* a long history of *film funning* discussed in this book, and silent film *can* provide opportunities for quick and dirty live scores that enhance public profile with minimal effort. I, however, advocate an approach, through musical means, that endeavors to uphold the *intentions and aspirations of the original film text*. This requires planning, preparation, and work.

As well as this opinionated approach, this book surely contains errors and omissions; there are always new discoveries and interpretations of historical records. I may have overlooked or misunderstood many things in film history, but the goal and purpose of this book is to inspire composers and performers to create *new* live scores that are entertaining, captivating, and yet true and faithful to the original films.

Integration with other texts

Silent film – its history, aesthetics, and influence – has been extensively researched. *Film music composition* is widely taught in academic programs and vocational workshops; ASCAP, BMI, and Sundance all offer highly competitive, mentored workshops.

What is *not* widely taught or researched is *the intersection of silent film and contemporary composition and performance*. Live scores, while popular, tend towards three pitfalls: (1) cliché imitations of perceptions of "silent film music," (2) expensive orchestral scores that demand many rehearsals or even click tracks, or (3) irrelevant, meandering jam sessions where the film is a backdrop for creative self-expression. This book explores other possibilities.

This book is intended to *complement*, not replace, existing film scoring and contemporary music composition texts or composition professors' private or group lessons. Readers may be familiar with composition texts by David Cope, Henry Cowell, Leon Dallin, Vincent Persichetti, and Arnold Schoenberg, to name a few.

Film scoring textbooks include *The Emerging Film Composer: An Introduction to the People, Problems, and Psychology of the Film Music Business* (2006) by Richard Bellis; *Complete Guide to Film Scoring: The Art and Business of Writing Music for Movies and TV* (Second Edition, 2010) by Richard Davis; and *On the Track* (Second Edition, 2004) by Fred Karlin and Rayburn Wright.

These are good upper division textbooks; their focus is the *Hollywood film industry*, rather than live performance or silent film. They share a *vocational* bent, appealing to students who want to "make it." They incorporate particulars ranging from technical details of dub stages to business psychology, self-help, and life coaching – Samuel Adler meets Donald Passman meets Tony Robbins. What they lack, for the composer and performer of *live scores*, includes history, aesthetics, cultural context, performance practice, and unconventional and improvisatory approaches, especially with regard to period silent film. This book covers those specialized areas.

Composing for Silent Film complements any of these books still in use today. It privileges a *live performance* aspect absent in these books, offering a model for *specialization* in live score performance. Rather than emphasizing conventional Hollywood industry practice, *Composing for Silent Film* encourages novel approaches in composition, conducting, improvising, and arranging.

In addition to university and conservatory students in film scoring programs, this book is intended to appeal to the *creative musician and improviser in the field*, already confident in their abilities, who seeks guidance in approaching silent film. This book aims to bring a better understanding of silent film to musicians and help composers plan and organize their scores.

Examples used

For clarity and concision, examples are limited to nine canonical silent films including: *Metropolis, Dr. Jekyll and Mr. Hyde, The Mark of Zorro, Sunrise: A Song of Two Humans, The Black Pirate, Nosferatu, The Phantom Carriage, Daisy Doodad's Dial*, and *The Golem*.

1 Silent film conventions

Audiences love silent film – ballets of light and shadow that transcend time. Contemporary audiences readily understand them – or *seem* to.

Contemporary audiences often miss subtle details of plot, character, and context, especially if these are not adequately reinforced in the accompanying score. (At the same time, aspects that may have passed unnoticed to period audiences may be glaringly obvious to contemporary audiences: misogyny, racism, xenophobia, unsustainability.)

Silent films employ conventions, some of which have been preserved in contemporary film, and some which have not. These conventions give meaning to silent film. Composers need to be aware of silent film conventions and consider them in their scoring. Composers should understand how a film played to an audience in its day, and how directors telegraphed meaning. Our goal is to *fully understand the film*, and to use an original score to help *our audience* grasp as much as possible.

Story, storytelling, plot, narrative, and themes

Let's briefly address some terminology that has been used, overused, applied and misunderstood: *story, storytelling, plot, narrative,* and *themes*. We distinguish these terms not just for purposes of discussion, but for how we *think about scoring a film*. (We should also acknowledge that the use of these terms has become slippery in public and even professional circles.)

Story is a basic, fundamental, underlying framework. It's the bare bones, the *spoilers*, what's left when superficial elements are evaporated, as one reduces a sauce in cooking. It is frequently *archetypal* in nature; Hollywood story archetypes include: boy-meets-girl; two buddies share a journey; a mysterious stranger comes to town and changes everyone's life. Story can be abbreviated and summed up quickly: think of the *elevator pitch*.

The ***story*** of *The Phantom Carriage* is: an inherently good, everyday man becomes an abusive drunk, but is redeemed through religious intervention. That's it. That's the story. That's *not*, however, why most people love the film. They love the film because of the ***storytelling***.

DOI: 10.4324/9781003254447-1

2 Silent film conventions

Storytelling is *how* a story is told. *The Phantom Carriage* tells a story through a series of flashbacks into the supernatural; it uses ghosts and horror, and mines anxieties of domestic abuse. It is this setting and treatment that is so engaging. Because ghosts and domestic abuse directly *support the story*, they are not gratuitous, and thus powerful.

Themes are recurring arguments and underlying messages explored or conveyed through the work. *The Phantom Carriage* has several prominent themes: the evils of alcoholism; the goodness of sacrifice, purity, and standing by your man; our earthly mortality. While expressed through ghosts and the supernatural, the central theme is that alcohol is bad; the film supports Sweden's prohibition movement at the time, which seems to be its ulterior motive.

Plot organizes story into acts, scenes, twists, and order of *exposition*. Plot is where elements of the story become arranged and rearranged: things that happened earlier may be presented later as flashbacks. Subplots and secondary storylines are placed in context. Plot can be *nonlinear*. Plot can have an *outline*. Plot can present *backstory* or omit unnecessary details, like where characters ate lunch.

Narrative, often used interchangeably with plot, implies *narration* and *narrator*; a story may be told from a particular *point of view*, and this viewpoint is crucial to narrative. Plot may diverge from narrative in cases where – considering *The Phantom Carriage* – intricate sequencing of flashbacks (or other devices) may be important to the *plot*, but less so to Sister Edit's personal narrative of self-sacrifice.

These distinctions matter; they inform our compositional choices in scoring a film. Should we hit some detail of the unfolding plot? Something that speaks to an archetypal story? Something that bolsters an underlying theme? A plot device? A character? A story element? Can we write music that supports several of these? In good situations, plot, themes, story, and narrative work together, enabling music to reinforce all of them. Still, there are always a number of musical paths and opportunities before you. There's more on this later in Chapter 2, Spotting: choosing what moments to play, and in Chapter 3, Plan your themes.

Exercises or thought experiments

What are some examples of a film in which two buddies share an adventure?

What are some examples of a film where a mysterious stranger comes to town and changes everyone's life?

Choose one of the primary example feature films from this book (or elsewhere).

1. In two or three sentences, condense the story of the film.
2. What are the major themes of the film?
3. What are some characteristics of the storytelling used?
4. What are some plot points, and do they relate to the theme or story? If so, how?

Advanced readers may note that these terms (story, storytelling, themes, plot, narrative) and their divisions rely heavily on *literary theory* and may question why they should be relevant to *cinema*. We may note that these concepts arise from western European literature, the elevation of Greek mythology, Plato, Aristotle, and "beginning-middle-end" structures that connect to "three act structure" – but this is *not* the be-all-end-all of storytelling. What *other* literary and visual traditions can be used to structure cinematic storytelling? What dramatic films exemplify non-western story structures?

Issues and cultural contexts of the silent period

Silent film conventions are *mechanical* – derived from the mechanisms or technical apparatus of filmmaking – and *cultural*, reflecting the zeitgeist, politics, and culture of the time and place they were made. This distinction helps us think about why some of these conventions are in place.

Mechanical conventions are, to varying degrees, inevitable and unavoidable. A shot is limited in duration by the amount of film held in the *magazine*; close-ups are limited by the focal length of the lens; contrast and saturation are limited by the lighting available and the sensitivity of the film; and so on. Mechanical factors may be somewhat variable: studio budgets determine the quality of the sets, the height of the crane, or the length of dolly track available to a production.

Cultural conventions are, to varying degrees, conscious and unconscious decisions: biases subtle or glaring, unquestioned cultural norms, prevalent moral values; the clothing, slang, and expressions of the time. There may be overt misogyny or dated social practices, like men opening doors for women. At the same time, women may be empowered in narratively significant ways: Ellen's superior knowledge and heroism in *Nosferatu*; the Wife's escape and agency in *Sunrise*; Daisy's superior skill in *Daisy Doodad's Dial*. There are dated social hierarchies, unapologetic and structural racisms, xenophobic ethnocentrisms, and ethnic caricatures (the opium den in *Dr. Jekyll and Mr. Hyde*; the Scotsman in *The Black Pirate*). Films test and suggest limits of acceptability and permissible points of view. Cultural conventions can be considerably more complex and nuanced than mechanical conventions. Music can amplify or downplay cultural conventions, and the composer must be aware of what is going on and sensitive to its emphasis or interpretation.

Mechanical conventions

Many characteristics of silent film derive from the capabilities of the equipment and techniques available at the time. How shots were composed or staged – including blocking, lighting, and camera movements – were aesthetic choices made within physical and mechanical limitations. A film's structure was formalized by editing and projection limitations.

Reels

Feature films were, by necessity, broken into *reels*. Projection alternated between *two* projectors; going back and forth intended to make reel changes seamless. Silent films were commonly projected at between 16 and 20 fps (frames per second); a full reel of 1,000 feet of 35mm film could yield up to 15 minutes.[1] Reel changes were placed where they would be less conspicuous, and often (but not always) aligned with scene changes.

Establishing shots

Camera shots at varying distances with varying *depths of field* were possible. An *establishing shot* might be a *wide shot* taken at a distance to show an exterior to communicate a scene's location. This convention continues today. Music can coincide with an establishing shot to help set things up, so the audience better understands the location. You might want music to communicate the location geographically (we're in France), or its relation to a particular character (this is Knock's office), for example. The establishing shot gives you a brief moment to set up a forthcoming scene.

Close-up

Mechanical conventions persist today: consider the close-up shot. Yet, close-ups are slightly different in silent film: camera lenses in use at the time didn't always have the focal length they do now. In many silents, close-ups were saved to show important plot points, such as the *reveal* of the Duke's signet ring in *The Black Pirate* (1926), for instance.

A close-up serves to visually magnify what is important. In a heavy-handed way, a close-up shot *forces our attention* on something that should not be missed (for reasons of plot), or is seen as a *pay-off* (voyeurism). This forcefulness – studied as the *male gaze* by scholars such as Laura Mulvey[2] – became the object of some criticism even during the silent period.

The close-up as a cliché

If you watch a play in live theater, everything you see is from the vantage point of your seat in the audience. In contrast, the close-up belongs to a particularly *cinematic visual vocabulary*. The close-up added novelty to the dramatic experience. Its use could really pop, and its overuse could wear out its welcome. A syndicated 1928 newspaper article, "The Movie Close-up," bemoaned the close-up as a cliché, particularly for prolonged kissing shots.

> Now that the Hollywood people are speaking out against the close-up movie clinches [sic], the time seems ripe for the launching of an anti-kissing movement all over the country. [...] [I]t was the directors who were to blame, and these are now coming around to understand that the non-stop kiss, photographed in slow motion close-up, has lost its thrill, if it ever had any.[3]

This article exhibits the prudishness that led to the censorial Motion Picture Production Code or "Hays Code."[4] But it also documents perceived *overuse of the close-up* in predictable moments or situations. Once technical issues were solved, and lenses with increasing magnification readily available, filmmakers enjoyed the ability to get in closer and closer, and could choose how often to change lenses.

For a composer, what does a close-up mean? When our *visual* attention is forcibly directed somewhere, the question arises: do we want to reinforce that musically? Does the shot need additional help? Or do we want to keep playing the scene as it was? Or should we indicate *something else* that's going on, like a reaction to or a distraction from a reveal? Is there a nuanced read to make, or does the music need to be "on the nose"?

Exercises or thought experiments

Find a short silent scene with a dramatic or important close-up.

Write a piece of music to accompany the scene.
Compose a version that hits the close-up hard.
Compose a version that hits the close-up subtly.
Compose a version that ignores the close-up.

What is the effect of each version?

---

6 *Silent film conventions*

Intertitles

Intertitles – *cards* with text on them for the audience to read – were a static interruption of the motion picture, and therefore kept to a minimum. This text is typically *dialogue* or some kind of *exposition*, stating time and place, for example, or backstory or context. Occasionally, intertitles establish structural moments in the film – the Acts of *Nosferatu*, for example.

During the silent period, these intertitles were actually called *subtitles* – a term that's now used for text burned through the bottom *lower-third* of the screen, such as for foreign translations. This burn through during the silent period would have required extensive, degenerative *composite optical printing*, and was avoided to preserve image quality. One might note the ragged quality of rudimentary dissolves in *Dr. Jekyll and Mr. Hyde* (1920) to see the sacrifices of early composite optical printing. Furthermore, intertitles allowed for very large text projected front and center in consideration of accessibility.

Today's subtitles tend to translate as much as possible. Period intertitles, by contrast, do not represent all speech, but just enough to clarify the gist of a conversation. Music performed in the cinema played through intertitles to smooth over the visual interruption. For foreign export, it was enough to swap out intertitles with those in a foreign language, simplifying what today is called *localization*.

Intertitles are a mechanical convention that clarifies the silent picture. A 1921 source estimated that "There are hundreds of them in a feature picture."[5] They were seen as necessary, but also part of the art of motion pictures. A 1921 article, "Writing in of Subtitles is Fine Art," posited

> So far, the director has been unable to tell his story without subtitle. [...] They play upon the imagination. They build a more vivid picture than the action of the film. They enhance the story told in the part of the film which follows the subtitle.[6]

On occasion, people have suggested to me that, using a video editing program (like Final Cut, Premiere, or Resolve), one could *remove* intertitles, tighten scenes, and add contemporary subtitles, to "improve" a silent film for live score performance. I strongly disagree with this idea! I believe that the integrity of a film should be preserved. Intertitles "build a more vivid picture" and are an integral part of the work.

Intertitles could solve *continuity* problems, where *coverage* was missing or shots didn't quite match. A 1918 newspaper explained:

> The sub-title is the reading matter thrown on the screen at the beginning or in the middle of a scene to bridge a break in the continuity or to emphasize

words or dialogue of a scene. It is sometimes called leader, sub-head or caption. They all mean the same.[7]

If continuity was problematic – for example, if actors had changed blocking, a light got moved, or a prop misplaced – the addition of an intertitle could distract from those mistakes. Still, our 1918 source advised:

> Have as few sub-titles as possible. It has been said that when the continuity of the picture drama will be so perfect as to dispense with all sub-titles, that will be the millennium of the motion picture. There is no rule, however, to govern the number of sub-titles. A forceful sub-title at the psychological moment will bring out your scene.[8]

It is noteworthy to read that a "forceful" subtitle could *improve* a scene. This may provide justification for a composer to, where appropriate, hit a *card* and punch it musically. Our source, in addition to recommending *fewer* subtitles, advises they should be *concise*:

> Much meaning must be expressed in a few words. People come to the picture house to see action, not to read it. [...] Remember, every word you put into your sub-titles costs the producer footage of the film, so express your ideas concisely without making the brevity too obvious.[9]

Note the issue of *cost*, an additional reason why intertitles were favored above subtitling through composite optical printing.

There's a practical reason for contemporary music makers to take note of intertitles. For a composer or ensemble, intertitles are useful topographical markers. In the not unlikely event a player (or whole ensemble) gets lost or misses a cue, intertitles clearly establish position in the film.

Exercises or thought experiments

Find a ten-minute *reel* or pick a short segment from a *contemporary sound film*.
Turn *off* the sound.
Write subtitles or intertitles for this segment, as if it were a silent film.
If you have a video editing system, try dropping in the cards!

How successful was adding interstitial cards?
If intertitling a contemporary film did *not* work out well, why not?
Is the silent era *photoplay* constructed differently from the photoplay of the talkies?
How are they different?

8 *Silent film conventions*

Cultural fascinations and conventions

Audiences often miss (or misunderstand) cultural references and social conventions in period silent film: allusions to actual events, news stories, literature, popular song or plays, but also commonplace period ideas, attitudes, protocols, and manners that reflect the cultural zeitgeist or tenor of the times. These didn't need to be spelled out for period audiences, but today, music can help frame or emphasize them.

Science and medicine

Consider that it was not until 1880 that Thomas Edison patented the electric light. Rapid technological growth and ambitious imagination closed the nineteenth century, when Auguste and Louis Lumière, Léon Gaumont, and others refined and publicly exhibited early motion pictures. Novelist H. G. Wells captivated readers with *The Time Machine* (1895), *The Invisible Man* (1897), *The War of the Worlds* (1897), and *The First Men in the Moon* (1901), exploring scientific ideas and speculating on their implied possibilities.

As audiences filled nickelodeons in the early twentieth century, scientific progress accelerated. German scientist Paul Ehrlich created the first synthetic antibacterial compound, arsphenamine, in 1907. Scottish scientist Andrew Fleming discovered penicillin in 1928. Advances in chemistry, poison gas, and methamphetamines fueled war machines.

These developments inspired and challenged popular imagination. Science was *not* widely taught in schools in the nineteenth century; the early twentieth century saw a push to add science curriculum to classrooms in the US and UK.[10] (One lasting legacy of the positioning of science outside education is the conflation of *science* and *industry*, which can be seen in the name of many museums.) A typical 1920 audience would likely have had very little, if any, scientific education, and the line between science and the wonder of magic was arguably more flexible than today. What may seem absurd now may have seemed plausible, or at least fascinating, to early audiences.

Dr. Jekyll and Mr. Hyde (1920) adapted for the screen Robert Louis Stevenson's 1886 novella, *The Strange Case of Dr Jekyll and Mr Hyde*. Stevenson was interested in transformation and in the contrast of good and evil that could reside within one person, and used a chemical serum as a dramatic device to explain and exaggerate those possibilities. The film connects with science, medicine, chemistry, and psychology, and exploits conservative distrust of those fields.

Dr. Jekyll, a doctor of medicine, owns a laboratory filled with equipment: beakers, Bunsen burners, test tubes, and other devices. Jekyll examines microbes under a microscope and informs his conservative colleague, "I tell you, Landon, we haven't <u>begun</u> to discover what science can do with the body and mind of man!" Dr. Landon, observing Jekyll's work, replies, "Damn it, I don't like it! You're tampering with the supernatural!" and warns him, "Stick to the positive sciences, Jekyll." This serves as *exposition* that Jekyll dabbles in potentially nefarious things, even if they are not specified to the audience: science can be potentially threatening and a gateway to the "supernatural." At this point in the film, we don't know who is right, Landon or Jekyll. Jekyll's lab becomes an important location, and his scientific work, while vague, explains ensuing events. As composers, we might think about how music might help audiences understand and navigate Landon and Jekyll's contrasting perspectives or how it might characterize Jekyll's laboratory.

In *Nosferatu* (1922), Professor Bulwer teaches his students "about the dreadful methods of carnivorous plants. One viewed with horror the mysterious workings of nature." A Venus flytrap catches a fly; quips the Professor, "Like a vampire, no?" *Parallel action* interrupts this scene: Knock, in prison, catches and eats flies, proclaiming, "Blood is life!" Back in Bulwer's study, under a powerful magnifying box, students view "a polyp with tentacles," devoured by another tiny creature, "little more than a phantom." We cut back to Knock, who watches a spider eat its prey. Music can guide an audience through this peculiar part of the film. Scoring *through these scenes* could *connect* them; giving them different music could differentiate them. What do they have in common? Why were they intercut? What do we want the audience to take away from these scenes?

These vignettes may *feel* extraneous and only superficially related to the rest of the film (or to each other). They may even feel like they distract from the narrative. We should understand *why* they are included, and, as composers, write music that relates them to the film, so the audience understands or infers why they are there. The very *invocation of science* serves to make the audience believe that there could be a plausible, logical explanation for vampirism, clairvoyance, and other fantastical phenomena. Music can help in this direction. Knock shows a telepathic connection to Orlock; this could be underpinned musically by referencing a theme that's tied to Orlock, vampirism, or blood. Bulwer demonstrates his expertise; the film needs to *establish* Bulwer as an expert in the sciences and medicine to support the plot. Music could paint Bulwer as a calm, respectable figure. The high magnification photography may look impressive, even futuristic, for audiences that had never peered through a microscope, and music could communicate a sense of wonder.

These sequences and techniques – Bulwer's fanciful dialogue, the invocation of science, futuristic imagery – support the *suspension of disbelief* and are still in use today: consider the *technobabble* and *visual effects* in shows like *Star Trek*. And as in *Trek*, music ought to reinforce the desired effect, regardless of scientific veracity. Imaginative sequences can challenge composers to find musical ways to keep the audience engaged and to reinforce onscreen *worldbuilding*.

10   Silent film conventions

Psychology

Sigmund Freud published *The Interpretation of Dreams* in 1899; Karl Jung published *Psychological Types* in 1921. Psychology expanded internationally, capturing public imagination.

Just as *Dr. Jekyll and Mr. Hyde* looked at transformation, good, and evil, Jung's concepts of *anima* and *animus* – feminine and masculine archetypes wrestling for balance in the unconscious mind – drive the Man's internal conflict in F. W. Murnau's *Sunrise: A Song of Two Humans* (1927). Murnau's Man – himself given only an archetypal name – struggles between extremes of violence and love, animosity and grace. The conflict in the film is nearly entirely psychological. The composer is challenged to make the Man's extremes real, make the events in the film believable, and to plumb the psychological depths and nuances presented in the film.

Influenza and disease

Themes of sickness and airborne disease permeate *The Phantom Carriage* (1921) and *Nosferatu* (1922), whose element of the Black Death – the European plague with no cure – would have resonated strongly with a 1922 audience that survived the Influenza Pandemic of 1918–19 that killed over 40 million people. *Nosferatu* has continuous references to mysterious airborne pathogens, and even a creepy microscope scene; this is no simple vampire movie.

The Phantom Carriage, based on a 1912 novel, uses alcoholism, consumption, and the transmission of disease as central plot points. Its morality play and prohibition stance hinge upon the real threat of fatal disease.

When disease is invoked in silent film, it alludes to the possibility of dire consequences, the severity of which may be accentuated musically for contemporary audiences.

Warfare and military technology

The Golem: How He Came into the World (1920) shows humanity losing control of a monster of its own making; this was interpreted as an allegory to World War One developments in weaponry, like armored vehicles, airplanes, and poison gasses. World War One, also called the Great War, raged 1914–18 and killed 8.5 million combatants and 13 million civilians. It was especially notable for skirting existing arms agreements, excessive deadliness, and cruelty.

Historian of war and popular culture, Michael Paris, in his introduction to *The First World War and Popular Cinema: 1914 to the Present*, argued that World War One shaped cinema in several ways. The motion picture enabled people to *see* the war through newsreels and other films, constructing a *dominant visual image* of the war. The war aided in the creation of *national (and nationalist) cinemas*, each with their own styles, funding, and studios, since the war fragmented the European continent and stymied international cooperation. *Propaganda* aspects of film became increasingly evident and exploitable. Images of wounded soldiers and dark technologies resonated with audiences.

The war cast a long shadow over cinema. Xenophobia and mistrust of foreign powers and distant lands appear in *Nosferatu* and *The Mark of Zorro* (1920). While xenophobia, wounded soldiers, and the horrors of warfare were not new, they were amplified by the extent of the conflict: some entire villages and graduating classes were wiped out, resulting in a "lost generation."[11]

While today's films may invoke war within the context of action, adventure, or superheroes, war in silent period films held additional gravitas given audiences' firsthand lived experiences, often on home soil. Nostalgic war humor later seen in shows like *Catch 22, Hogan's Heroes*, or *M*A*S*H* is uncommon during the silent period.

In "Orchestrating War," contemporary American film composer Carter Burwell noted the persistence of tropes like brass, drums, and marches to describe war, as well as rousing or uplifting music used to encourage public enthusiasm for conflict.[12] Burwell was *observing* musical stereotypes, rather than advocating their continued propagation. There are many possible ways to score references to war. During the silent period, the public was more likely to feel fatigue than enthusiasm for war. Composers should recall the weight and import of war in the silent era and carefully consider whether war should be played as tragic, heroic, comic, or with some subtle, nuanced interpretation, to help a contemporary audience get the right idea.

Exercises or thought experiments

Consider ways in which war might be portrayed, musically or narratively, without being maudlin or relying on jingoism or nationalism. How is war glorified musically? How is war portrayed as tragedy musically? How does different music affect onscreen portrayals of wartime and warfare?

For any particular film – especially a silent film – how can you ascertain a director's intentions or sympathies in the portrayal of war? How can those sympathies be reinforced musically?

Take a look at *The Golem*, especially before man loses control of him. He appears kind of like a pet or a giant robot. Can you write some music that implies the danger he represents, without being too heavy handed, or giving away the plot?

12 Silent film conventions

Racism and colonialism

Handling overt racism in silent film remains a challenge for contemporary exhibition. Some films may be too problematic to redeem – consider *The Sheik* (1921) starring Rudolph Valentino, wherein Arabs are a dangerous and barbaric race to be conquered and restrained. Although this film launched an iconic leading man to stardom, it may be inappropriate for public screening today.

Racial stereotypes and historical revisionism were designed for the benefit of white audiences (presumed to be the bulk of ticket buyers) and to justify society's structural oppression and white privilege. During the silent period, race humor and "Lost Cause" narratives dominated cinema, as they did magazines, books, and theater.[13] Racist stereotypes and humor demeaned blacks, but also Arabs, Jews, Chinese, Hispanics, and Indigenous peoples, as well as, in some American films, othered Europeans including Spaniards, Irish, Italians, and other immigrants.[14]

Efforts to start black motion picture companies in the US were stymied by a lack of funding and "confusion among blacks about what message they wanted to convey." Black film companies were often "partly, and sometimes wholly, owned and run by whites and simply made low-budget films using Hollywood themes with black casts." Some adopted an "uplift formula":

> The race movies of the 1920s reflected the ambitions of the black bourgeoisie who produced them. They urged black audiences to aspire to middle-class values and status, retailing black Horatio Alger success myths and condemning the corruptions of ghetto existence.[15]

Such 1920s silent race movies coincided with the Harlem Renaissance and the New Negro Movement; these films had to negotiate shifting cultural (and commercial) divides and differences of opinion about representation, realism, and idealism. The "uplift formula" could be problematic, misrepresenting the harsh severity of insurmountable, real-life obstacles, and promoting an assimilationist, capitalist agenda. These Horatio Alger myths were not the types of progress everyone wanted glorified.

Depiction of mixed-race people was tellingly offensive. Actor, writer, and critic Peter Noble, recalling "The Negro in Silent Films" in his landmark 1948 book, *The Negro in Films*, wrote:

> In all the films made during this period dealing with octoroons and mulattos the apparent shame and degradation of being even in the smallest degree non-white was exploited to the full, with the obvious implication that there was something practically sub-human in being black. Indeed, in several productions the lesson seemed to be that for the unfortunate

mulatto only suicide provided a logical escape from a world in which to be partially coloured was considered an even worse disgrace than to be a full-blooded Negro.[16]

Scholarship by Henry T. Sampson, Donald Bogle, Lester D. Friedman, and other film historians provides a wealth of additional guidance that composers may consult for greater information and analysis. Ultimately, racism, colonialism, and other dated bigotry force us to consider whether certain films are suitable for general public exhibition at all.

Programming suitability

Questions that *this* book must address include which films are acceptable to perform, how to handle problematic scenes musically, and what should inform those decisions.

Films whose basic premise or worldview is racist are best avoided. Many scholars uphold *The Sheik* or *The Birth of a Nation* as examples of *technically* advanced filmmaking, but captive general audiences cannot see technical achievement without being subjected to triggering racism or being manipulated to identify with racist protagonists. These films are best left for academic study than public performance. The *worst* films are not difficult to spot. Many others are harder to judge.

For films that teeter on the margins of acceptability or have limited problematic parts, there are a number of approaches. Consult the affected: if a film stereotypes a particular ethnicity, go to that community and request guidance. Remember, you can always choose to simply *not* do the film. I argue films should be screened unaltered; it is not faithful to history or to cinema to excise offending bits, even if you own the editing software to do so. Efforts to sanitize (or abridge or colorize) film have been met with contempt, as they only whitewash problematic bits, covering up difficult sections that deserve our scrutiny.

If you decide to do a particular film, it is true that you can always give an introduction before the performance and explain what people will see. I consider this given. I wish to entertain *musical* possibilities within your score: it is not enough to simply make excuses to an audience; one must handle difficult scenes with delicacy.

While we cannot deny onscreen racism, we should not purposefully accentuate it either. I would caution composers to track other things transpiring in a scene, or aim for a more subdued reading. *Don't* play racist caricatures and jokes. While this may deviate from filmmakers' original intentions, they won't land. Let them slide; find something else to hit.

Consider the opium den in *Dr. Jekyll and Mr. Hyde* – probably the most problematic scene in an otherwise relatively inoffensive film. This vignette presents a number of Chinese or "oriental" stereotypes in bit parts in the opium den. Rather than accentuating Chinese stereotypes, a better musical approach is to hit the drug-induced stupor and narcotic vibe, or to keep the music focused on Jekyll/Hyde's descent into sinfulness. There is enough going on that you don't need to resort to gimmicky "Chinese music."

One might consider the phenomenon of new opera productions that attempt to set problematic or ideological texts into contemporary environments, and to offer new or different insights into the text. This is a difficult analogy because, without altering the film itself (again, not advised under any circumstances), the visual element takes precedence to an audience. Music may distract but cannot erase overtly offensive racism or sexism.

Misogyny and gender roles

Silent films frequently show dated attitudes towards gender as well as outright misogyny. In *The Sheik*, women are men's property, and if a man takes a woman by force she will fall in love with him. No surprise if we decide *not* to score this film.

Other films are more complex, demand a closer look, and allow a composer to finesse a delicate approach. *Nosferatu* on its face reinforces stereotypical gender roles: men work and are heads of the household. At the same time, leading man Hutter is a bit of a nitwit while his wife Ellen is perceptive and smart. Ultimately, it is *Ellen* who defeats Count Orlock, having a better handle on the situation than her husband (and two esteemed doctors who are characterized as the town's wise men). Hutter grabs more screen time but ultimately has less agency than Orlock, Knock, or Ellen herself.

Similarly, in Murnau's *Sunrise: A Song of Two Humans*, the Man may be physically stronger, but the Wife is more intelligent, perceptive, and emotionally mature.

In these films, a composer has opportunities to highlight the women, to emphasize their agency, and to play scenes from their point of view. The women often carry different experiences, motivations, or outlook in a scene, and this could well be the angle that a composer chooses to score.

Exercises or thought experiments

Find a scene with a man and a woman, or both male and female characters. Write two summaries of the scene: one as you imagine it perceived by a male character, and one as you imagine it from a female character's point of view. Consider the differing musical opportunities each summary suggests.

Note, this exercise can be performed for any two characters of different backgrounds.

Queerness

Cinema historian Vito Russo noted that early silent films contained numerous portrayals of homosexuality, from "the harmless sissy" comedic stereotype, to titillating lesbian innuendo, to effeminate foils (or punching bags) for violent and fragile masculinity. There *were* contrasting films that were provocative, celebratory, advocative, or that presented gender nonconforming or nonbinary people, such as *Different from the Others* (1919, Germany, *Anders als die Andern*) or *Salomé* (1923). Hitchcock's *The Lodger* (1927, UK) initially presents the hero as "queer" but as a "gentleman" nevertheless (ca. 00:31:30). As much as Russo accentuated period homophobia, his research reveals broad international representation of a variety of perspectives, some bigoted, some less so.[17]

The spectrum of queer representation, even if opaque at times, provides opportunities for interpretation or highlighting. Consider the homosocial male environment of *The Black Pirate* and its parade of scantily clad, muscular sailors.[18] What is the basis for all that camaraderie?

Another fascinating example is the homoeroticism of Count Orlock's bloodlust for young Hutter in *Nosferatu*. This is not unintentional; Russo noted that F. W. Murnau was a gay director who sublimated his sexuality into subversive horror and fantasy films.[19]

It would be disastrous to play these moments in a musically campy way. Dropping a disco beat might be funny, but it would tank the director's intentions, something I advocate against, even if *film funning* is a practice with a long history and its own fans.

I encourage you to use awareness of queerness in silent film to develop rich, deep, layered, and complex understandings and musical portrayals of characters and situations. There has been a tendency for contemporary scores to treat silent film as monochromatic and simplistic. Music can suggest greater depths and broader interpretations. The benefit of this approach is that it will make your presentation of a film more compelling.

Acting style

This section examines highly stylized acting methods seen in silent films. Studying silent film acting helps us correctly interpret story, character motivations, and a director's intentions. We can then apply this understanding to our musical score. Subtleties of acting performance create musical opportunities for composers who recognize them.

Early magic lantern and picture shows showcased *movement*, rather than text. Subsequent motion pictures evolved from these visual forms; motion pictures developed within the context of scientific and technological innovation, yet maintained ties to pantomime and theater. Silent films employed stylized acting methods, replete with exaggerated gestures. These acting styles were carefully studied and performed.

16 Silent film conventions

Because filmmakers tried to transmit as much information as possible through *performance* without leaning too heavily on intertitles, a dramatic, communicative acting style was preferred, largely based on the Delsarte System of Expression and other nineteenth-century theatrical approaches, such as those developed by Benoît-Constant Coquelin, Émile Jaques-Dalcroze, Sir Charles Bell, and even Charles Darwin. A schism in nineteenth-century schools of theatrical acting put "controlled" acting in opposition to "inspired" acting; "controlled" acting won out, connecting acting to science, discipline, and practiced performance, and this influenced cinema internationally.

One might observe that France was home to both the development of the motion picture (the Lumière brothers; Gaumont, the first film company) and the art of the mime. It's easy to assume that miming therefore influenced cinema acting style; there is some truth to this, but the story is more complex.

François Delsarte's System of Expression predated film and endeavored to *catalog and define* dramatic gestures. The telegraphing of information through oversized gestures proved highly useful for film. Similarly, Dalcroze imagined Wagner's *German* operas performed in Paris in an era before supertitles, and he developed ways to coach opera singers to act and gesture so a *French* audience could understand the drama. This objective easily extended to acting for silent film, so that film actors could be understood without audible speech.

The scientific cataloging of motion and gesture, the notion of acting as technology, the correlation of poses or "attitudes" with emotions, and the desire for "controlled" acting, all aligned to shape acting style in silent film.

Delsarte

Well before the advent of film, French singer and acting coach François Delsarte (1811–71) gained international prominence. During the technology-fascinated nineteenth century, Delsarte attempted to catalog the many "attitudes" or poses of the body, with special attention given to the arms, face, and hands. This was seen as a *scientific* endeavor.[20] Delsarte was a charismatic coach and public speaker; he could be rambling, impromptu, and vague, and although he didn't actually publish much himself, he made people think about what to do with his catalog of poses.

In the United States, Delsarte's thoughts were transcribed, translated, and written up by Genevieve Stebbins in 1885.[21] *Delsarte System of Expression* was "translated from unpublished manuscripts."[22] Stebbins translated Delsarte's French word *attitudes* as "attitudes," rather than "poses" – the simpler, more accurate, literal translation – probably because "attitudes" sounded more scientific and erudite. Heavily illustrated, the book describes poses, movements, and exercises.

These poses or "attitudes" were numerous and complex. Figure 1.1 catalogs some of the positions of the head. Imagine that an actor might train to

Silent film conventions 17

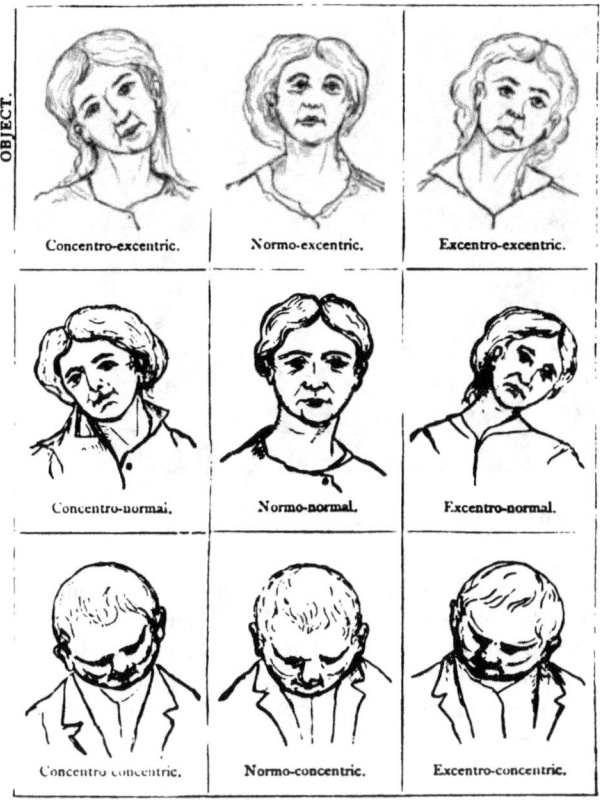

Figure 1.1 "Attitudes of the Head." Stebbins (1885) p. 135.

move between these positions, while being aware of each one. Figure 1.2 is a still frame from Murnau's *Sunrise: A Song of Two Humans*. Actress Janet Gaynor tilts her head, trying to get the Man's attention. Does her pose correlate to any of the Delsarte attitudes?

Delsarte parsed the eye into descriptions of the brow, the upper lid, the lower lid, and the eyeball itself. "By combining nine of the brow with nine of the lid eighty-one distinct combinations can be made."[23] Figure 1.3 shows nine "simple combinations of upper lid and brow." Compare these to the film still, Figure 1.4, where character actor J. Farrell MacDonald, as The Photographer

18 *Silent film conventions*

Figure 1.2 The Wife tilts her head in *Sunrise*.

in *Sunrise*, arches his brow dramatically in a *reaction shot*. How would you describe his mood? What do you think he might be thinking?

Delsarte described combinations of gestures and important body movements. He attempted to *codify functions and meanings* associated with specific gestures and movements. "The functions of the hand" were listed:

1. To define or indicate;
2. To affirm or deny;
3. To mold or detect;
4. To conceal or reveal;
5. To surrender or hold;
6. To accept or reject;
7. To inquire or acquire;
8. To support or protect;
9. To caress or assail.[24]

Accompanying these functions were a variety of instructions for movement. These instructions coached the actor, for example, "To conceal: bring the palm of the hand toward you, the fingers at the same time gently closing on palm."[25] This gesture can be seen in many silent films; Figure 1.5 shows a

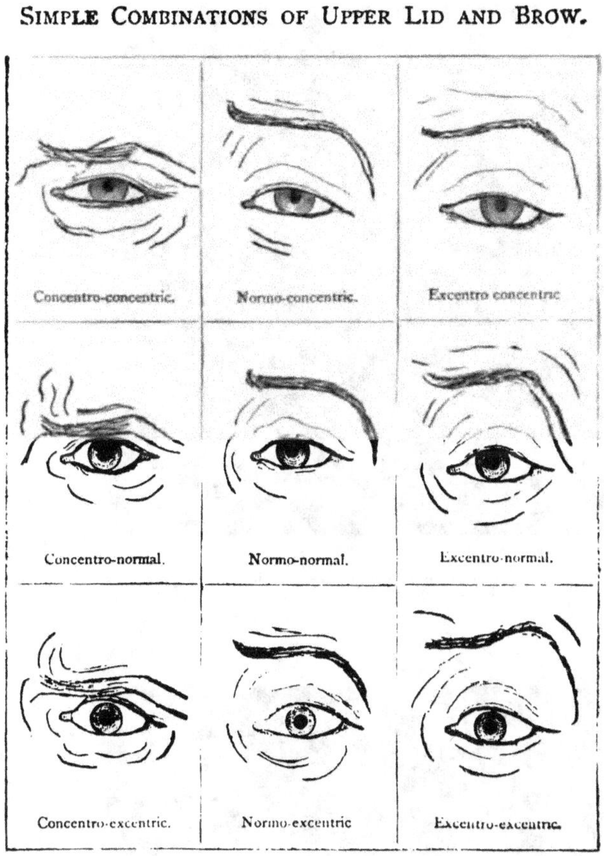

SIMPLE COMBINATIONS OF UPPER LID AND BROW.

Figure 1.3 "Simple Combinations of Upper Lid and Brow." Stebbins (1885) p. 152.

close-up of this concealing gesture performed by actor Sam De Grasse in *The Black Pirate*. Figure 1.6 shows some of Delsarte's attitudes of the hand, including the closed fist.

Some Delsarte movements may look stagey or awkward, but nevertheless were used in silent film: "To reject: fingers unclose from down-turned palm as if throwing something away."[26] John Barrymore can be seen performing this gesture (Figure 1.7) in his conflicted persona in *Dr. Jekyll and Mr. Hyde* (1920), rejecting the impulse to take the potion. Even if this gesture is uncommon in daily life, its theatricality is effective communication, even today. Picking up on these gestures helps us as composers to grasp meaning in silent film.

20 *Silent film conventions*

Figure 1.4 The photographer in *Sunrise* reacts to a comic moment.

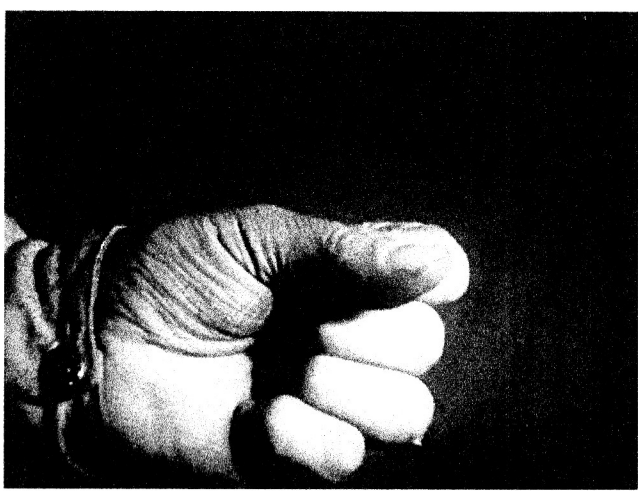

Figure 1.5 The Black Pirate. The Lieutenant closes his fist around the short straw.

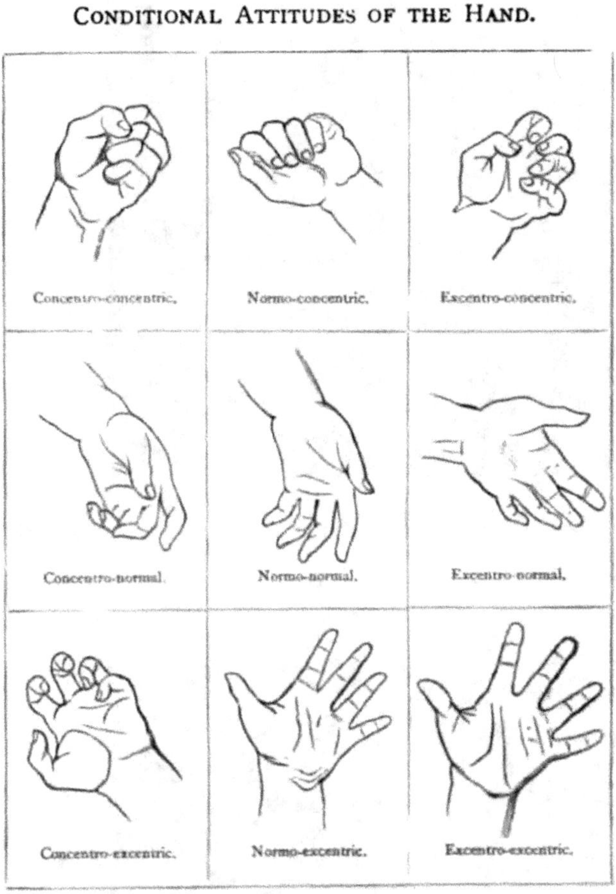

CONDITIONAL ATTITUDES OF THE HAND.

Concentro-concentric.	Normo-concentric.	Excentro-concentric.
Concentro-normal.	Normo-normal.	Excentro-normal.
Concentro-excentric.	Normo-excentric.	Excentro-excentric.

Figure 1.6 "Conditional Attitudes of the Hand." Stebbins (1885) p. 97.

Exercises in *Delsarte System of Expression* are placed throughout the book, which was intended to be used like a workbook, not just read. The exercises coach making movements and instruct their dramatic implementation. Some of these exercises do include brief texts, to emphasize movement's meaning:

> Exercise XIV. Place your hand on your heart, the moral or affectional zone, and repeat: "Or this true heart with treacherous revolt turn to another."[27]

This gesture appears often in silent film. In this reaction shot (Figure 1.8) from *Metropolis* (1927), Freder, seeing Maria's entrance, clasps his hands to

22 Silent film conventions

Figure 1.7 Dr. Jekyll rejects the impulse to take the potion. *Dr. Jekyll and Mr. Hyde* (1920).

Figure 1.8 Freder sees Maria. *Metropolis* (1927).

Silent film conventions 23

Figure 1.9 Florian and Miriam share a passionate moment in *The Golem* (1920).

his heart, a symbol of his falling in love. (Note how his companion poses to hold him back, advising restraint). The same gesture appears in *The Golem* (Figure 1.9), where Florian and Miriam share a passionate moment, their hands indicating their mutual love. It's important to note that this gesture is not gendered. Both men and women made this gesture.

Delsarte was internationally influential well beyond the nineteenth-century theatrical period during which he cataloged gestures. His work is now in the public domain, and many more illustrations and diagrams can be found online. I recommend these not because a composer needs to learn all these gestures, but because a composer will benefit from realizing the depth and extent to which acting was studied and structured.

Exercises or thought experiments

Try these fun acting exercises from Delsarte's teachings, as related by Genevieve Stebbins (1887).

Place your hand on your forehead, the mental zone, and say, "There's a fearful thought!" (p. 49)

> *Resigned Appeal to Heaven.* (a) Right shoulder raises slightly, while head sinks in opposition; (b) upper arm makes rotary movement, which turns eye of elbow out; (c) then forearm unbends; (d) hand expands in tenderness; head has been slowly rising in opposition and is right, oblique, back, when movement ceases. (p. 117)
>
> *Remorse.* Hand decomposes, then forearm; this drops hand on back of head, which has risen in opposition to meet it; eye of elbow to front. (p. 117)
>
> Dilate and contract the nostrils as rapidly as possible; move no other portion of the face. (p. 158)
>
> Imaginary Scene IX. You glance toward object. To your amazement, another transformation has taken place. A vision of beauty is before you. Great astonishment depicted on face. You are attracted toward vision. It recedes. You beseech it to remain with you, but it vanishes, leaving you prostrate. (p. 183)

Dalcroze

Swiss composer and educator Émile Jaques-Dalcroze (1865–1950) created an educational system eventually known as "eurhythmics" that used movement to teach musical arts from ear training to gesture for opera performance. Dalcroze developed what he called "Rhythmic Gymnastics" (in contrast to Delsarte's "Aesthetic Gymnastics"[28]) throughout the 1890s while teaching at the Conservatory of Music in Geneva. In 1906, his influential book *Méthode Jaques-Dalcroze: Gymnastique Rythmique* was published in French and German.[29] Figure 1.10 shows a classic Dalcroze Rhythmic Gymnastics exercise, which emphasizes body control and coordination.

While Dalcroze focused on acting for *opera*, his ideas influenced direction for cinema. Dalcroze thought that acting should follow *rhythm*, a pretty straightforward idea for opera, and one that extrapolated well to silent film. Dalcroze wrote:

> Just as verbal expression, the poetic interpretation of the text, demands precise and definite gestures, so *musical* expression, constituting the atmosphere of the piece, exacts of the actor a similar and absolute physical submission to the rhythm that produces it.[30]

Dalcroze supplied theory and practice to Delsarte's catalog of gestures, emphasizing that dramatic interpretation demanded "precise and definite" gestures; these gestures could communicate meaning in situations where text was obscured (because it was sung in a foreign language, for instance). So,

Figure 1.10 Limb Independence Exercise. Jaques-Dalcroze (1906) p. 114.

if you could communicate Wagner opera to a Francophone audience through gestures, imagine what you could do with silent cinema.

Other educators and theorists built on a foundation laid by Delsarte and Dalcroze. French composer, musicologist, and critic Jean d'Udine (1870–1938) wrote a 1910 book, *Art and Gesture*, bearing the inscription, "All art forms are a series of poses; every artistic creator is a specialized mime."[31] The book includes a chapter that addresses "cinematic arts" whilst focusing on music and decorative arts.[32]

Mikhail Yampolsky, a scholar of Russian and Slavic studies, discussed the influence of Delsarte and Dalcroze on Russian filmmakers:

> Delsarte's ideas began to penetrate Russia at the very beginning of the twentieth century. [Delsarte's teaching] achieved real popularity around

1910–1913 when the former director of the Imperial Theatres, Prince Sergei Volkonsky, became its propagandist. He published [...] several books giving a detailed exposition of the new acting system.[33]

Yampolsky noted that "the Volkonsky–Delsarte–Dalcroze system had a fundamental significance for film theory at the beginning of the 1920s" and had "elements that were later used by filmmakers."[34]

Dalcroze's *Rhythm, Music, and Education*, published in English in 1921, further spread his ideas and methods. Jo Pennington's *The Importance of Being Rhythmic* (1925) applied the theories of Dalcroze to music, dancing, and acting, including an entire chapter on "Eurythmics and the Actor."

Controlled acting

Jo Pennington advocated "Controlled Acting,"[35] an approach promoted by Benoît-Constant Coquelin (1841–1909), a French actor of tremendous prominence who wrote extensively about acting and theater. In a section titled "Controlled Emotion of the Actor,"[36] Pennington directly quotes Coquelin, who in 1880 described a schism in acting philosophy:

> The theatrical world is divided into two opposing camps in regard to the question whether the actor should partake of the passions of his rôle, – weep, to draw tears, – or whether he should remain master of himself throughout the most impassioned and violent action on the part of the character which he represents; in a word, remain unmoved himself, the more surely to move others.[37]

Both "opposing camps" didn't make it through to be enshrined in cinema. "Controlled acting" won out over "inspired acting" (as Pennington called it), and for good reason. Coquelin, years before cinema, described the advantages of controlled acting:

> This is why the true actor is always ready for action. He can take up his part, no matter when, and instantly excite the desired effect. He commands us to laugh, to weep, to shiver with fear. He needs not wait until he experiences these emotions himself, or for grace from above to enlighten him.[38]

Coquelin says "the true actor is always ready for action"; this would prove especially important in cinema when cameras roll and the director shouts, "Action!" The film actor must perform on command.

Pennington, quoting Coquelin, described "Controlled Acting":

> Acting, then, is not the hit-or-miss inspirational performances that press-agents would have us believe. It is an art which depends upon the actor's

ability "to remain unmoved himself, the more surely to move others"; upon a conscious direction of his forces – nerves, muscles, sensibilities – the medium through which he must express himself.[39]

These "nerves, muscles" reflect the poses described by Delsarte and a focus on anatomy described by Sir Charles Bell, discussed further below. Pennington emphasized pitfalls of "inspired" acting, presenting an argument paraphrased directly from Coquelin:

> It is as unnecessary for the actor to be moved as it is for a pianist to be in the depths of despair to play the 'Funeral March' of Chopin or Beethoven aright. He knows it; he opens his instrument and your soul is harrowed. I would lay a heavy wager that if he should give way to any personal emotion he would play but ill. By analogy, an actor who regards his own emotions otherwise than as material is likely to fare badly. It is therefore my opinion a mistake to trust to inspiration. Nothing is more likely to produce inspiration than good, hard preparatory work.[40]

Similarly, if you play your musical live score to a silent film, you do not need to be in the "depths of despair" to play a sad theme or moment.

The allegory comparing acting to musicianship appeared in other acting books of the time, such as *Screen Acting* (1922). A chapter on "The Mechanics of Emotion" describes controlled acting based on scientific research and methodology:

> [T]he technique of the actor bears much the same relation to his finished performances as five finger exercises and scales bear to the playing of a concerto. Technique is the scientific equipment of the actor – the framework on which his work is built. And it's this science – the mechanics of emotion – that every young actor must study diligently if he would build his career on a firm foundation.[41]

In keeping with the fascination with *science*, here acting, too, is placed within a scientific paradigm "that every young actor must study diligently." *Screen Acting* cites and recommends other scientific sources to support its arguments:

> Fortunately there are men who had spent their lives in observing the effect of various emotions on men and animals and the results of their investigations have been published and are available to students of acting. Probably the most widely read book on this subject among professional actors is "The Anatomy and Philosophy of Expression" by Bell. And another source of much helpful information on this subject is Darwin's "Emotions in Man and Animals."[42]

28 Silent film conventions

Sir Charles Bell (1774–1842) was trained in painting, anatomy, and surgery. His *Essays on the Anatomy of Expression in Painting* (1806) stressed the importance of understanding anatomy when depicting expression. A second edition titled *Essays on the Anatomy and Philosophy of Expression* came out in 1824. The third edition, published posthumously in 1844, was expanded and entitled *The Anatomy and Philosophy of Expression as Connected with the Fine Arts*. New editions came out every few years throughout the century, such was its influence and popularity.[43]

Illustrations and essays in Bell's book describe in detail the expression of a wide variety of emotions and reactions: laughter, weeping, grief, pain, fear, despair, jealousy, joy, rage, remorse, madness, and others. This book formed a template for actors. Compare Figure 1.11, "Fear with wonder" from Bell to John Barrymore's expression (Figure 1.12) as his potion proves successful in *Dr. Jekyll and Mr. Hyde*.

Screen Acting pointed readers to Bell's book – written when, like Delsarte, cataloging expression was seen as a scientific, technological pursuit – and then recommended applying these gestures in a systematic, controlled way. *Screen Acting* critiqued the "inspired" acting decried by Pennington:

> The person who "acts all over the place" does not succeed in making the audience feel the emotion which he is portraying; he simply makes himself

FEAR with WONDER

Figure 1.11 "Fear with wonder" in Bell (1844) p. 148.

Silent film conventions 29

Figure 1.12 John Barrymore reacts to the success of the potion in *Dr. Jekyll and Mr. Hyde* (1920).

absurd. To know just which are the significant movements that will convey an emotion's poignant appeal, to use these, and no others – that is one of the secrets of emotional acting.[44]

Screen Acting advocated studying movements from Bell and Darwin, selecting them judiciously, and then using them in a controlled technique to convey emotion, rather than just acting out. The thinking was that *science* determined these poses and gestures, and therefore, that's what the actor should learn and perform.

Bell thought that emotions and emotive expressions were uniquely human. Charles Darwin did not agree and responded in his own 1872 book, *The Expression of the Emotions in Man and Animals*.[45] It's fascinating to see evolutionary theorist Darwin thrust forward as a guide for actors, but so he was. Furthermore, *Screen Acting* took Darwin's text verbatim as a source for acting exercises: "Following is his list of questions, a list that should be carefully studied."[46] Some of these questions appear below as Exercises.

Exercises or thought experiments

Try these acting exercises from *Screen Acting* (1922) which are directly taken from Charles Darwin's *The Expression of Emotion in Man and Animals* (1872 pp. 15–16).

30 Silent film conventions

> 1. Is astonishment expressed by the eyes and mouth being opened wide, and by the eyebrows being raised?
> 3. When a man is indignant or defiant does he frown, hold his body and head erect, square his shoulders and clench his fists?
> 9. Is contempt expressed by a slight protrusion of the lips and by turning up the nose and with a slight expiration?
> 13. Do children when sulky pout or greatly protrude the lips?

Comedy

Comedic acting was physical and demanding. *Daisy Doodad's Dial* (1914), directed by and starring Florence Turner, uses a "face making competition" as a setup to showcase Turner's abilities. Turner pulls her face in multiple expressions and contortions, crossing and circling her eyes (Figure 1.13). These comedic expressions were rehearsed to perfection; like silent dramatic gestures, they are not haphazard.

Inez and Helen Klumph, authors of *Screen Acting*, wrote of the demands of comedic acting:

> [Comedian and actor] Ben Turpin believes that the most important requisite of a comedian is a supple, expressive body. The absurd postures

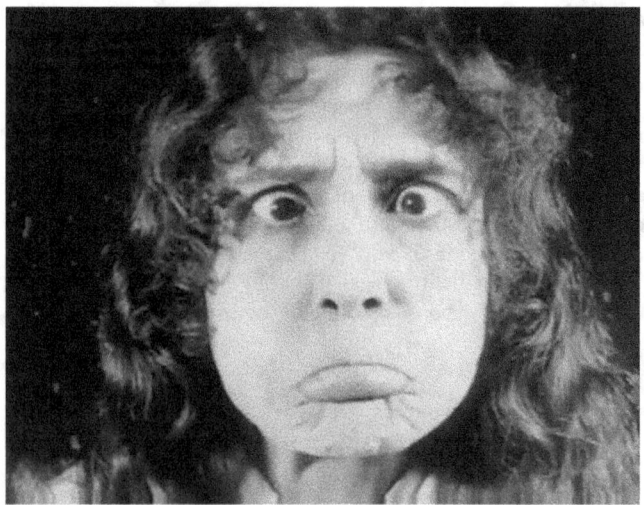

Figure 1.13 Florence Turner makes a face in *Daisy Doodad's Dial* (1914).

he strikes are not accidental by any means; they are each and every one worked out before a mirror.[47]

Physical acting was an important part of silent comedy. Dry wit and wordplay are less common in silent film than in sound film; silent film excels in slapstick, screwball comedy, parody, physical comedy, and comedies of errors. Yet audiences today often miss things in silent films that were meant to be funny.

Sunrise is upheld as such a sacred, watershed film that composers and audiences often miss the funny bits: the runaway pig, the drunken cook, the couple's ignorance of the Venus de Milo, the flirtatious old man at the end. Similarly, many bit parts in *The Black Pirate* are quite comical, even if the overall film is a swashbuckling adventure.

You should be aware of intentional comedy in films. As a composer considering musical approaches, you may wish to downplay it, accentuating the underlying narrative; or you may wish to really yuk it up. A comedic moment may need help, or it may not. But you should recognize it when it's there.

Exercises or thought experiments

Find a silent *dramatic* film. Watch closely for moments of comedy, and choose two or three. (They can be short and subtle.)

1. Why are they in the film? Do you get a sense of comic relief, or not? Do they feel realistic within the world of the film?
2. Consider different ways of scoring them. How much emphasis could you give them? Try writing two to three different musical options for each one. Do they detract from the film? Do they make these little moments pop? Can you overdo it? If you score through without hitting the comedy, what is the effect? What works best in each case, and why?

Acting and your original musical score

This section presents a lot of historical information about silent film acting. As composers, what should we do with this information?

While audiences today may find Delsarte's broad gestures blatant and unsubtle, it's remarkable how often they are missed or misunderstood. Hands over the heart can mean love; hands clasped can mean desire, pleading, or desperation; a hand to the forehead can mean dizziness, illness, fainting, being overwhelmed, and so on. Hundreds of these gestures were standardized internationally. It is important that musical score acts in congruence with characterizations and emotions presented in actors' gestures.

D'Udine, Dalcroze, Volkonsky, and others correlated gesture and emotion. This was especially important in silent film: if an actor couldn't *speak* their thoughts, they could *indicate* them through gesture. This practice was seen as technical and theoretical. Technically, there was a lexicon of gestures that could be learned and memorized; these gestures informed acting technique. Theoretical aspects, dating to Bell and Darwin, correlated gestures and movements to emotions; Dalcroze and d'Udine theorized connections between movement, rhythm, and all the arts.

Observe silent film acting closely and conscientiously. Notice gestures, and consider possible meanings. Notice how elements of pantomime or gesticulation are incorporated, and what they suggest about character, internal dialogue, and motivations. Notice how *controlled acting* is implemented; if a gesture seems exaggerated or stagey, consider how this is deliberate and what it is intended to signpost. When gestures *shift* – for example, the Wife in the rowboat in *Sunrise* (ca. 00:29:00) weighing her situation – notice how this reveals the complexity of a situation, or something changing, or perhaps human inconsistencies. These observations should give you a better reading of a film, and help guide the creation of a faithful musical score.

Exercises or thought experiments

Find a short scene or sequence, about two minutes long, which has two to three characters using controlled acting with clear gestures, and preferably few or no intertitles.

1. Create a script for the imagined or implied dialogue.
2. Write down a hypothetical *interior monologue* for each character.

Find a short scene or sequence in a screenplay from a sound film.

1. See if you can use standard silent film gestures to tell the story without spoken dialogue.
2. Are there new contemporary gestures (like dabbing, for example) that might be incorporated? What are their meanings?

Special effects

Silent films are rich with *special effects*; ingenious tricks and trade secrets vividly brought to life the fantastic and the surreal. There were no computer graphics or digital intermediates, but there *were* possibilities of increasingly complex *composite optical printing* (as seen in *Sunrise: A Song of Two Humans*). Music can work with special effects to make them more believable and compelling.

Raymond Fielding, in his iconic mid-century manual of special effects cinematography, classified special effects in three ways: in-camera effects, laboratory processes, and combinations of the two.[48]

With *in-camera effects*, audiences saw onscreen something actually seen and filmed through a camera. Fielding described basic in-camera effects as changes in speed, position, or direction; image distortions; optical transitions; superimpositions; and day-for-night photography. Image replacement effects include split-screen photography, in-camera matte shots, and shots made using glass or mirrors. The use of miniatures is an in-camera special effect.

Laboratory effects include bi-pack printing, optical printing, traveling mattes, and aerial image printing. These effects were done in the laboratory with film negatives. *Combination techniques* include background projection, using either rear or front projection.

I lack space to explain special effects in depth; one authoritative discussion of silent era special effects is "The Evolution of Special Visual Effects" in *The ASC Treasury of Visual Effects*.[49] For the purposes of this book, we consider how special effects might impact our musical score.

Special effects were compelling to period audiences *not* because they were fooled into thinking some spectacle had *actually happened*, but because it was something they had *never seen before*. There was no standard of comparison for movie magic. The grotesque giant spider in *Dr. Jekyll and Mr. Hyde* (ca. 01:08:40) is unsettling even today, although it looks far from real; special effects artist George E. Turner called this "one of the most terrifying moments in silent cinema."[50] It deserves to be amplified musically, rather than mocked as camp.

The magic of special effects, at its best, helps advance the narrative, rather than being gratuitous. Even if an audience recognizes a special effect, the *suspension of disbelief* makes the film more enjoyable. In a critique of underwater sea swimmers in *The Black Pirate* (ca. 01:25:20), a period reviewer noted:

> The audience may scream with laughter at the ridiculous situation of hundreds of men swimming under water without a bubble rising to the surface, but they applaud, as well.[51]

Your audience may applaud as well if you play special effects sequences as if they are real, treating them with the intention to help create the desired effect. If hundreds of men are meant to be swimming underwater, you can make *environmental sounds* (discussed in Chapter 2) that will help place them (and the audience) in watery surroundings. Whatever the special effect is, you may be inspired to create music that bolsters the effect and the story around it.

> **Exercises or thought experiments**
>
> Find a short scene or sequence with some kind of special effect, model, or optical effect.
>
> 1. Write some music that *imitates or follows* the special effect itself.
> 2. Write some music that *downplays or ignores* the effect, for example, focusing on a character, emotion, theme, or situation, anything germane apart from the special effect itself.
> 3. Write some music that tracks the special effect's *narrative purpose*; in other words, it doesn't quite imitate the effect, but tries to bolster whatever situation called for the effect to be used.
>
> What is the effect of each approach? In what circumstances is one approach better than another?

Editing conventions

Understanding film editing and awareness of editing techniques helps inform our decisions in creating a musical score that connects with a film.

In his book, *In the Blink of an Eye: A Perspective on Film Editing*, Oscar-winning editor Walter Murch explained how silent period editing relied on memory and an intuitive sense of time. Editing tools back then were rudimentary compared to later sound-era machinery – such as the Moviola, Steenbeck, or KEM – which in turn were superseded by today's computer systems. Murch compared the silent era editing room to a "tailor's shop":

> In the first quarter of the twentieth century, the film editor's room was a quiet place, equipped only with a rewind bench, a pair of scissors, a magnifying glass, and the knowledge that the distance from the tip of one's nose to the fingers of the outstretched hand represented about three seconds. In those manual, pre-mechanical days – roughly 1900–1925 – the cutting room was a relatively tranquil tailor's shop in which time was the cloth.[52]

The editing process was laborious, requiring good memory and intuition. "Manual," of course, means film editing was done directly by hand; mechanical systems took over towards the end of the silent era (Murch estimates by 1925; note that late silent films are technically advanced, and early sound shoots often simplified to accommodate clunky new sound equipment). Murch continued his description of the 1900–25 period manual film editing:

The editor had seen the film projected when it first came from the laboratory, and now she (many editors in those days were women) re-examined the still frames with a magnifying glass, recalling how they looked in motion, and cut with scissors where she thought correct. Patiently and somewhat intuitively, she stitched the fabric of her film together, joining with paper clips the shots that were to be later cemented together by a technician down the hall.

She then projected the assembly with the director and producer, took notes, and returned to her room to make further adjustments, shortening this and lengthening that, like a second fitting of a suit. This new version was projected in turn, and the cycle was repeated over and over until the fit was as perfect as she could make it.[53]

While flatbed editors (and now computers) replaced scissors, the *language* and *techniques* of film editing were *already in use* in the silent period: establishing shots, exteriors preceding interiors, master shots, montages, parallel action, close-ups, match cuts, visual rhythm and pacing, matching *eye trace* between shots – a shared editorial practice allows us to treat silents like contemporary film.

Composing and performing *live music* for silent film is likewise laborious, requiring good memory and intuition, especially if you eschew click tracks and computers. The benefit of live human synchronization is that it forces you to be and play in the moment, and I believe that audiences sense that excitement and mental concentration.

Bridging transitions

Editing for narrative film frequently adheres to a storytelling syntax established during the silent era. To show a *scene* – a concept itself derived from the theater – a standard sequence of shots might begin like this: an *establishing shot*, often an *exterior* shot, shows us where the scene takes place. An interior shot brings us inside. A *master shot* – a single continuous take of an entire scene, showing all the actors within the frame – is interspersed with close-ups, reaction shots, and medium shots that help break up visual monotony and tell the story in a more engaging way. The pacing of these cuts establishes a visual rhythm.

Music can help smooth and bridge these cuts and transitions. The visual rhythm might help suggest a tempo for the music, how fast or slow the scene should feel. Music can also help smooth and bridge transitions in and out of subsequent scenes. Chapter 2 *Scene divisions* discusses transitions between scenes in greater detail. Music can lead us gently into a new scene, can smooth a rough edit, and can help make a scene's ending feel conclusive.

> **Exercises or thought experiments**
>
> Find a short sequence with a change of scene. Look closely at the scene change.
>
> 1. Write music that ends with the first scene, and a new piece that begins with the second scene.
> 2. Write music that ends *before* the scene change, and a new piece that starts *early*, so it *prelaps* or *leads us into* the next scene.
> 3. Write music that *lingers* across the scene change, ending as we are already into the next scene.
> 4. Write music that takes the third approach, but that affects some kind of musical transition to mark the scene change.
>
> Which approach worked best? What made it work, or not work? Would a different set of scenes yield different results? What are some factors that might affect the choice of approach?

Music's role in continuity

Continuity is a major concern in filmmaking. The concept, often fluidly applied, relates to how film mimics the continuous temporal flow of everyday life: events unfold in a proper order; time passes in a logical and consistent manner; people don't suddenly appear in different clothes mid-scene; props don't magically appear or disappear mid-scene. Even how continuity is manipulated in surrealism, flashbacks, or flashforwards is a continuity concern itself. Continuity is often taken for granted, until there are mistakes; these can occur especially when there are *pick-ups* or reshoots. Continuity errors are frequently cited as "film goofs" on IMDb.com and other film websites.

Filmmaker and theorist Raymond Spottiswoode, in discussing "the psychology of cutting" in *Film and Its Techniques*, differentiated between what he called "dynamic cutting" and "continuity cutting," both of which date to the silent period.

Dynamic cutting, "developed in classical Russian silent films like *The Battleship Potemkin*," "largely disregards the regular continuity of story cutting, and substitutes the film's particular ability to relate together things which may have occurred far apart."[54] Dynamic cutting can yank the spectator abruptly through time and space with powerful effect.

Spottiswoode contrasted this with continuity cutting, which has a "recognizable continuity of movement and dialogue. Carried to extreme lengths, this would mean that a film would simply reproduce a stage play, with little or no change of angle or introduction of parallel action."[55] Spottiswoode cast these approaches as ideological extremes; "in practice, cutting has come to be a combination of dynamic cutting and continuity cutting."[56]

Music can help preserve continuity across *jump cuts* or other ragged edits; a bed of music reinforces continuity throughout a scene. Music can emphasize other aspects of continuity such as location, time, and character when cutting becomes more dynamic.

The edit may jump back and forth between distant locations, showing events happening simultaneously; this is called *parallel action*. In *Nosferatu*, Count Orlock in the Carpathian Mountains somehow entrances Ellen back in Wisborg (ca. 00:34:00). Music *could* emphasize the different locations, or it could flow continuously, gluing the scenes together, emphasizing that *this is all happening at the same time*. In this case, music emphasizes temporal continuity.

The edit may jump back and forth in time, like in *Dr. Jekyll and Mr. Hyde* when we visit old Italy (ca. 00:36:00), or in *The Phantom Carriage* where we see flashbacks and alternate realities (ca. 00:46:20; ca. 00:59:30). In these cases, music might distinguish the present from other time periods, helping to orient the audience within a *nonlinear narrative*.

In some cases, locations might have their own particular music or musical style; we might musically contrast The City and the countryside in *Sunrise*, where this dichotomy is of thematic and narrative importance. Such musical contrasts could be useful to distinguish different but similar locations, such as the different ranches in *The Mark of Zorro*. In this case, you are providing helpful continuity based on location.

The Black Pirate has a large ensemble cast of similar pirates; these pirates are distinguished by details of clothing, hairstyle, props, hats, and mannerisms. Music could help distinguish between different pirates, giving a unique flavor to MacTavish, the Powder Man, and the Peg Leg pirate.

Composers should consider music's power to glue things together or to distinguish them. This applies to picture editing, whether that leans more toward dynamic cutting or continuity cutting or a mixture of both. How can music reinforce the desired effects of the picture edit?

Exercises or thought experiments

Find a short sequence with parallel action.

1. What is happening in each location?
2. Why are these two (or more!) locations being intercut? What is the purpose, meaning, or message of the parallel action?

> 3. Write some music that changes for each location.
> 4. Write some music that stays consistent throughout the sequence.
>
> Which approach works better? Why? Can you combine or moderate the approaches?

Editing tricks

Beyond bridging transitions and reinforcing continuity, editing can create cinematic sleights of hand. Author and photographer Kalton C. Lahue discussed editing tricks used in fight scenes in silent serials – exciting, one-reel shorts that often ended in a cliffhanger so audiences would return to the theater to see the next episode. A director wanted punches to come fast and heavy.

> What we saw on the screen was given impact and speed by an editing trick. The cutter removed every third or fourth frame from the sequence which showed moving fists. Used in moderation, this technique produced realistic effects when projected.[57]

Editing techniques were implemented in conjunction with special effects – like the in-camera change of film direction mentioned previously – to augment their effectiveness. Here Lahue describes how a devastating blow was safely staged:

> [In order to capture a] conclusive blow, the cameras were stopped. Both men took up predetermined positions at the edge of the cliff and Bart leaned backward as far as possible. Freddie placed his fist on Bart's jaw and let it rest there lightly. With the cameras turning backward, he suddenly pulled it away. [...] A rapid cut-in view from another angle, usually below and at a distance, showed a dummy or stuntman representing Bart going over the cliff to his doom. Carefully handled, it was most effective.[58]

The net effect of this sequence is to show Freddie punching Bart so hard he reels off a cliff. It's a good example of how editing works in tandem with special effects and multiple angles to achieve the desired effect. Music can help add excitement and match the quick pace of the action.

Lost and damaged footage

Editorial issues and concerns confront us as we score silent film: shots may be missing or reordered; restorations may be incomplete; damaged frames may have been dropped. Scenes may have been deleted during the Hayes Code era or in conservative territories. Much lost footage is unrecoverable, but music has an opportunity to suggest what has gone missing or smooth over a jagged visual.

Exercises or thought experiments

Find a short sequence that appears to have damaged or missing frames, or is somehow jagged or jerky, or seems to suggest lost or missing footage.

1. Write some music for this sequence.
2. Watch it with and without the music.

How well does music help improve the film? Do different kinds of music do a better job at covering the damaged footage?

Notes

1 The talkies standardized 24fps because of the need for increased fidelity for sound. See Kawin, Bruce F. (1992). *How Movies Work*. pp. 46–7. (Berkeley, CA: University of California Press).
2 See Mulvey, Laura. (1989). *Visual and Other Pleasures*. (London: Palgrave Macmillan).
3 *Democrat and Chronicle*. "The Movie Close-up." November 27, 1928. Page 16. (Rochester, NY).
4 See especially Schumach, Murray. (1964). *The Face on the Cutting Room Floor: The Story of Movie and Television Censorship*. (New York: William Morrow and Company).
5 *Des Moines Tribune*. "Write a Sub Title for Movie and Win Prize." December 7, 1921. Page 1. (Des Moines, IA).
6 *The Winnipeg Tribune*. "Writing in of Subtitles is Fine Art." November 26, 1921. Screen, Page 1. (Winnipeg, Manitoba, Canada).
7 Philpott, Robert. "Movie Contest Leads." *The Sacramento Star*. July 25, 1918. Page 2. (Sacramento, CA).
8 Ibid.
9 Ibid.
10 Del Giorno, Bette J. "The Impact of Changing Scientific Knowledge on Science Education in the United States since 1850" in *Science Education*, Vol. 53, Issue 3 (1969), pp. 191–5.
11 Winter, J. M. "Britain's 'Lost Generation' of the First World War" in *Population Studies*, Vol. 31, No. 3 (Nov., 1977), pp. 449–66. (Taylor & Francis, Ltd.).
12 Burwell, Carter. "Orchestrating War" in *Harper's*, February 2004, pp. 15–19.
13 Woll, Allen L., and Miller, Randall M. (1987). *Ethnic and Racial Images in American Film and Television: Historical Essays and Bibliography*. (New York: Garland Publishing, Inc.). p. 40.
14 Ibid.
15 Ibid. pp. 39–44.

16 Noble, Peter. (1948). *The Negro in Films*. (London: Skelton Robinson). p. 29.
17 Russo, Vito. (1981). *The Celluloid Closet*. (New York: Harper & Row). pp 7–30.
18 Consider Mel Brooks' interrogation of the homosexuality of background studio contract actors presented in the "French Mistake" sequence of *Blazing Saddles*, discussed in Dubowsky, Jack Curtis. (2016). *Intersecting Film, Music, and Queerness*. (Basingstoke: Palgrave), pp. 208–23.
19 Russo, Vito. *The Celluloid Closet*. 1981. (New York: Harper & Row). p. 52.
20 Delsarte, François. (1887). "Delsarte's Address Before the Philotechnic Society" in *Delsarte System of Expression*, Second Edition by Genevieve Stebbins. (New York: Edgar S. Werner). p. LIV.
21 Stebbins, Genevieve. (1885). *Delsarte System of Dramatic Expression*. 1886. (New York: Edgar S. Werner). See copyright notice date on first edition.
22 Stebbins, Genevieve. (1885). *Delsarte System of Expression*. Second Edition. 1887. (New York: Edgar S. Werner). See title page.
23 Ibid. p. 153.
24 Ibid. pp. 89–90.
25 Ibid. p. 90.
26 Ibid. p. 91.
27 Ibid. p. 52.
28 Ibid. pp. 12, 28, 40.
29 Jaques-Dalcroze, Émile. (1906). *Méthode Jaques-Dalcroze: Gymnastique Rythmique*. (Neuchâtel: Imprimerie Delachaux & Niestlé S. A.).
30 Jaques-Dalcroze, Émile. (1921). *Rhythm, Music, and Education*. Translated by Harold F. Rubinstein. (New York: G. P. Putnam's Sons). p. 200. (Emphasis in original.)
31 d'Udine, Jean. (1910). *L'art et le geste*. (Paris: Librairies Félix Alcan et Guillaumin Réunies). (Translation mine.)
32 Ibid., pp. 87, 279.
33 Yampolsky, Mikhail. (1996). "Kuleshov's Experiments and the New Anthropology of the Actor" in *Silent Film*. Edited and with an introduction by Richard Abel. (New Brunswick, NJ: Rutgers University Press). p. 46.
34 Ibid.
35 Pennington, Jo. (1925). *The Importance of Being Rhythmic: A Study of the Principles of Dalcroze Eurythmics Applied to General Education and to the Arts of Music, Dancing and Acting. Based on and Adapted from "Rhythm, Music and Education" by Émile Jaques-Dalcroze*. (New York: G. P. Putnam's Sons). p. 99.
36 Ibid., p. 96.
37 Coquelin, C. (1880). *L'art et le comédien*. (Paris: Librairie Paul Ollendorff). p. 27; Also in Coquelin, C. (1881). *The Actor and His Art*. Translated by Abby Langdon Alger. (Boston, MA: Roberts Brothers). p. 26.
38 Coquelin (1881) p. 28.
39 Pennington (1925) p. 99.
40 –Pennington (1925) p. 97; this paraphrases Coquelin (1881) pp. 31–2.
41 Klumph, Inez and Helen. (1922). *Screen Acting: Its Requirements and Rewards*. (New York: Falk Publishing Co., Inc.). p. 125.
42 Ibid., p. 126.
43 Hughes, Sean and Gardner-Thorpe, Christopher. (2022). "Charles Bell's (1774–1842) Contribution to Our Understanding of Facial Expression" in *Journal of Medical Biography*. DOI: 10.1177/0967772020980233
44 Klumph, Inez and Helen. (1922). p. 194.
45 Darwin, Charles. (1872). *The Expression of the Emotions in Man and Animals*. (London: John Murray).
46 Klumph, Inez and Helen. (1922). pp. 127–8.
47 Ibid., p. 200.

48 Fielding, Raymond. (1972). *The Technique of Special Effects Cinematography*. Third Edition. (London and Boston, MA: Focal Press).
49 Turner, George E. (1983). "The Evolution of Special Visual Effects" in *The ASC Treasury of Visual Effects*. Edited by George E. Turner. (Hollywood, CA: American Society of Cinematographers).
50 Ibid., p. 36.
51 *The Boston Globe*. "Douglas Fairbanks in 'The Black Pirate.'" May 11, 1926. Page 25. (Boston, MA).
52 Murch, Walter. (2001). *In the Blink of an Eye: A Perspective on Film Editing*. Second Edition. (Los Angeles, CA: Silman-James Press). p. 75.
53 Ibid., pp. 75–6.
54 Spottiswoode, Raymond. (1951). *Film and Its Techniques*. (London: Faber and Faber). p. 104.
55 Ibid., p. 105.
56 Ibid., p. 105.
57 Lahue, Kalton C. (1968). *Bound and Gagged*. (Cranbury, NJ: A. S. Barnes and Co., Inc.). pp. 121–2.
58 Ibid., pp. 122–3.

Bibliography

Altman, Rick. (2008). *A Theory of Narrative* (New York: Columbia University Press).
Bell, Sir Charles. (1806). *Essays on the Anatomy of Expression in Painting* (London: C. Whittingham).
Bell, Sir Charles. (1824). *Essays on the Anatomy and Philosophy of Expression* (London: John Murray.)
Bell, Sir Charles. (1844). *The Anatomy and Philosophy of Expression as Connected with the Fine Arts* (London: John Murray) (This is considered the Third Edition; it is followed by other editions, including: Fourth Edition (1847) (London: John Murray); Sixth Edition (1872) (London: Henry G. Bohn).
Bell, Sir Charles. (1885). *The Anatomy and Philosophy of Expression as Connected with the Fine Arts*, Seventh Edition, Revised (London: George Bell and Sons).
Bogle, Donald. (2001). *Toms, Coons, Mulattoes, Mammies, & Bucks: An Interpretive History of Blacks in American Films*, Fourth Edition (New York: Continuum).
The Boston Globe. (1926, May 11). "Douglas Fairbanks in 'The Black Pirate.'" (Boston, MA), p. 25.
Burwell, Carter. (2004, February). "Orchestrating War." *Harper's*, pp. 15–19.
Coquelin, C. (1880). *L'art et le comédien* (Paris: Librairie Paul Ollendorff).
Coquelin, C. (1881). *The Actor and His Art*. Translated by Abby Langdon Alger (Boston, MA: Roberts Brothers).
Darwin, Charles. (1872). *The Expression of the Emotions in Man and Animals* (London: John Murray).
Del Giorno, Bette J. (1969). "The Impact of Changing Scientific Knowledge on Science Education in the United States Since 1850." *Science Education*, Vol. 53, No. 3, pp. 191–5.
Democrat and Chronicle. (1928, November 27). "The Movie Close-Up." (Rochester, NY), p. 16.
Des Moines Tribune. (1921, December 7). "Write a Sub Title for Movie and Win Prize." (Des Moines, IA), p. 1.

Dubowsky, Jack Curtis. (2016). *Intersecting Film, Music, and Queerness* (Basingstoke:Palgrave), pp. 208–23.
d'Udine, Jean. (1910). *L'art et le geste* (Paris: Librairies Félix Alcan et Guillaumin Réunies).
Fielding, Raymond. (1972). *The Technique of Special Effects Cinematography*, Third Edition (London and Boston, MA: Focal Press).
Friedman, Lester D. (1982). *Hollywood's Image of the Jew* (New York: Frederick Ungar Publishing Co.).
Hughes, Sean and Gardner-Thorpe, Christopher. (2022). "Charles Bell's (1774–1842) Contribution to Our Understanding of Facial Expression." *Journal of Medical Biography*. DOI: 10.1177/0967772020980233
Jaques-Dalcroze, Émile. (1906). *Méthode Jaques-Dalcroze: Gymnastique Rythmique* (Neuchâtel: Imprimerie Delachaux & Niestle S. A.).
Jaques-Dalcroze, Émile. (1921). *Rhythm, Music, and Education*. Translated by Harold F. Rubinstein. 1921 (New York: G. P. Putnam's Sons).
Kawin, Bruce F. (1992).*How Movies Work* (Berkeley, CA: University of California Press).
Klumph, Inez and Helen. (1922). *Screen Acting: Its Requirements and Rewards* (New York: Falk Publishing Co., Inc.).
Lahue, Kalton C. (1968). *Bound and Gagged* (Cranbury, NJ: A. S. Barnes and Co., Inc.).
Mulvey, Laura. (1989). *Visual and Other Pleasures* (London: Palgrave Macmillan).
Murch, Walter. (2001). *In the Blink of an Eye: A Perspective on Film Editing*, Second Edition (Los Angeles, CA: Silman-James Press).
Noble, Peter. (1948). *The Negro in Films* (London: Skelton Robinson), p. 29.
Paris, Michael. (1999). *The First World War and Popular Cinema: 1914 to the Present* (Edinburgh: Edinburgh University Press).
Pennington, Jo. (1925). *The Importance of Being Rhythmic: A Study of the Principles of Dalcroze Eurythmics Applied to General Education and to the Arts of Music, Dancing and Acting. Based on and Adapted from "Rhythm, Music and Education" by Émile Jaques-Dalcroze* (New York: G. P. Putnam's Sons).
Philpott, Robert. (1918, July 25). "Movie Contest Leads." *The Sacramento Star* (Sacramento, CA), p. 2.
Russo, Vito. (1981). *The Celluloid Closet: Homosexuality in the Movies* (New York: Harper & Row).
Sampson, Henry T. (1977). *Blacks in Black and White: A Source Book on Black Films* (Metuchen, NJ: The Scarecrow Press).
Sampson, Henry T. (1998). *That's Enough Folks: Black Images in Animated Cartoons, 1900–1960* (London: The Scarecrow Press).
Schumach, Murray. (1964). *The Face on the Cutting Room Floor: The Story of Movie and Television Censorship* (New York: William Morrow and Company).
Spottiswoode, Raymond. (1951). *Film and Its Techniques* (London: Faber and Faber).
Stebbins, Genevieve. (1885). *Delsarte System of Dramatic Expression*, 1886 (New York: Edgar S. Werner).
Stebbins, Genevieve. (1885). *Delsarte System of Expression*, Second Edition, 1887 (New York: Edgar S. Werner).
Turner, George E. (1983). "The Evolution of Special Visual Effects." In *The ASC Treasury of Visual Effects*. Edited by George E. Turner (Hollywood, CA: American Society of Cinematographers).

Winnepeg Tribune. (1921, November 26). "Writing in of Subtitles is Fine Art." Screen [section] (Winnepeg, Manitoba, Canada), p. 1.

Winter, J. M. (1977, November). "Britain's "Lost Generation" of the First World War." *Population Studies*, Vol. 31, No. 3, pp. 449–66 (Taylor & Francis, Ltd.).

Woll, Allen L. and Miller, Randall M. (1987). *Ethnic and Racial Images in American Film and Television: Historical Essays and Bibliography* (New York: Garland Publishing, Inc.), pp. 39–44.

Yampolsky, Mikhail. (1996). "Kuleshov's Experiments and the New Anthropology of the Actor." In *Silent Film*, Edited and with an introduction by Richard Abel (New Brunswick, NJ: Rutgers University Press).

2 Consider your film

Studying and understanding a period silent film is the first step towards creating a new score. A nuanced, accurate reading of silent film facilitates a compelling original score.

This book argues that a live score works best when it supports the film, when film and music work *together*. Silent film can and has been exploited as a visual backdrop for musical self-indulgence or noodling. But for an audience, such navel-gazing will never be as compelling as when *story* and *visual image* are centered and uplifted by carefully crafted music.

Filmmakers and musicians have advocated this film-centric approach as long as there has been film itself. A popular weekly periodical, *The Moving Picture News*, advised musical accompanists in 1911:

> In order to properly play for pictures, you must at all times consider that you are a part of the audience, and watch intently for every little detail or suggestion that will help you lend that atmosphere of realism to the picture.[1]

The stated goal here is to create a musical "atmosphere of realism" so that the audience will be absorbed into the film. The way for the accompanist to do this is to become aware of "every little detail or suggestion" that is part of the film. This requires a great deal of study, especially with a feature-length film. You will need to watch the film many times to catch all its details and suggestions.

There's a number of ways to watch, study, and understand a silent film. All are beneficial and can provide insights that will inform your musical score. As you stay open to interpretations, certain ideas may resonate with you and suggest ways music can support the film. Studying the film *increases your options*, offering a wider variety of musical possibilities from which to choose than if the film is merely a visual backdrop.

As we look at a variety of ways to watch and understand a film, consider how each might suggest musical approaches.

DOI: 10.4324/9781003254447-2

Formalist reading

A *formalist reading* privileges the original film as text, focusing attention on the world created *within the film*. Without sinking too deep into film theory, here are some important takeaway points.

British film scholar Ian Christie, in discussing "Formalism and neo-formalism," noted that formalism "was born, historically, of the desire to find an objective or scientific basis for literary criticism."[2] This objectivity was found *within the text itself*. Christie explained, "Formalist critical tools are still used [...] by film theorists concerned with analyzing the structure of narration."[3] Formalists made a distinction between "story" and "plot" (as discussed in Chapter 1); the story being "an imaginary sequence of events" while the plot "provides the actual narrative pattern of the work, or 'story-as-told.'"[4]

Formalism suggests that focusing on the "story-as-told" will help us arrive at an "objective" interpretation of the film. Prioritizing a careful formalist reading – rather than a clever reinterpretation – approximates how a professional media composer works with a director today: respecting the director's intent and vision. Imagine that it is your job to understand and support a silent film's director's *original vision* as it is suggested by the film itself.

Consider F. W. Murnau's *Nosferatu*. Many *other* vampire films centering Dracula were made after *Nosferatu*. They do not matter. Corny tropes of bats and garlic pedaled heavily in later films should not be a point of reference.

A composer *could* reinterpret *Nosferatu* in a clever way: maybe Knock is the *good guy* trying to save Orlock's dying race from extinction – but that's not Murnau's *Nosferatu*. While that might be a novel interpretation, it disrespects *Murnau's* film, as would playing the film for laughs. At the same time, some musical scores gloss over truly comedic moments in *Nosferatu*: Knock hiding behind a tree stump, or a dockworker trying to smash a rat that bit him. So, a score that *only* sees *Nosferatu* as dark and heavy is likewise missing the "story-as-told." (Comedy is further discussed in Chapter 3.)

A formalist reading helps situate a new score *within* the director's vision and *within* the world created by the film, rather than commenting on it from without. The importance of formalism and recognizing where comedy is appropriate – and where it is not – brings us to a brief digression on the practice of *film funning*.

Film funning

This book actively discourages *film funning*, a period practice in the silent era, where cinema accompanists, typically pianists or organists, would use music to *mock* a film. These accompanists would choose inappropriate musical selections that used jokey references or deliberately clashed with filmmakers' intentions. Descendants of this approach include Carl Stalling's musical quotations in Warner Bros. cartoons, and the *Mystery Science Theater 3000* comedy series. Note that Stalling's musical witticisms served to broaden the appeal of children's cartoons that were *already comedies* to adults and to expedite his scoring process by recycling existing compositions.[5]

Disdain for film funning dates as early as its implementation. In 1911, *The Moving Picture News* advised accompanists:

> Do not at any time try to burlesque a picture or produce comedy yourself where none is intended, as it only cheapens the value of your music to those who know how it should be played – and the others will like any kind you play.[6]

The Moving Picture News reiterated this stance in subsequent issues.[7] A multitude of reasons justify their advice: film funning deflates or devalues the film; any music suffices as long as it shits on the film for laughs; it doesn't contribute to the cinematic experience; it takes the audience out of the film; it exploits low hanging fruit musically and comedically. Film funning, while a persistent temptation to novices today, fell out of favor with the rise of the feature film.[8]

Another argument against film funning today is the idea of *stewardship*. A composer should bear some responsibility towards creators long passed who can no longer defend their work themselves. Copyrights have long expired; deceased filmmakers cannot exert creative control over what you do or how you exploit their work. While this gives us opportunities to create new scores (and some room to create our own readings of a film), we should also act as good stewards of a work, to preserve or enhance its reputation, and encourage others to enjoy and respect it.

Exercises or thought experiments

Choose a sequence from a silent film that is *not* a comedy.

1. Try doing some of your own film funning. See if you can mock the film. See if you can work counter to the director's intentions. See if you can poke fun at it using musical references.
2. How easy or difficult was this? What was the effect? Would an audience enjoy it scored this way? What would be gained or lost?
3. Score the sequence without film funning. Does the film seem as silly? Is the film any more or less entertaining? Are there places where film funning is appropriate? Would different audiences respond differently?

Apparatus theory

The concept of *apparatus theory* is that film is a construct of the *apparatus of filmmaking*: all its machinery and machinations. Film music appears *within* that apparatus, not as an external discourse (another argument against film funning). Music should complement the camera angles, shots, and edits that are the building blocks of filmmaking. *How* a film was shot, edited, and is ultimately manifested depends upon film's apparatus: particular equipment (its capabilities and limitations), organizational structures (their workflow and production processes), even systems of finance and exhibition (studios, financiers, investors, and distributors).

Who has *access* to that apparatus makes film *ideological*: often capitalist, racist, sexist, homophobic, reinforcing a sociopolitical status quo. Experimental filmmaking *may* escape some of that, giving us incentive to seek out experimental silent film, and yet such films still exist within *technical limitations* – consider *Man with a Movie Camera* (1929) by Soviet filmmaker Dziga Vertov. The film showcases Vertov's innovations, drawing attention to the filmmaking apparatus.

As you watch a film in preparation to score it, be aware of the apparatus of filmmaking, and how that shaped the film: from ideological biases, to casting, to the height of a *crane shot*, to the length of a *dolly shot*, to the number of *extras*. Eventually, how *you* compose and perform your score becomes part of that apparatus as well.

Studying cultural context

While the *formalist reading* discussed above suggests that all you need to know already resides within the film itself, this is too simplistic. Formalism is an interesting ideal, but the idea that we know it all just because we watched the film is sure to fail us. It is vital to study the historical *cultural context* of a film, especially as regards themes and messages to which period audiences would have been sensitive.

The Phantom Carriage (Sweden 1921) is a spooky, speculative, supernatural thriller. Even a formalist reading of the film highlights recurring themes that imply cultural context; there are reasons why themes were chosen and so heavily stressed. The film's brutal depiction of alcoholism coincided with prohibition movements. In 1922, a Swedish national referendum narrowly failed to prohibit alcohol, with 51% voting against the ban. Recurring themes of airborne illness and the flu resonated strongly with an audience that survived the Influenza Pandemic of 1918–19 that killed over 40 million people.

The Influenza Pandemic similarly overshadows *Nosferatu*, spelled out in an introductory title card: "an Account of the Great Death in Wisborg." Vermin aboard the ship concern the crew and dockworkers because the rats may carry the plague. In one scene – whose inclusion can baffle today's audiences – Professor Bulwer and his students observe microbes under a microscope as he lectures. The scene appeals to period fascinations with scientific and medical progress, but it also characterizes Bulwer as an *expert* always ready with a *scientific* explanation. The scene paints him as a knowledgeable authority, perceptive but *not* superstitious. At the end of *Nosferatu*, Bulwer is foregrounded, deep in thought, as Hutter mourns his dead wife, Ellen. *Within the film*, Bulwer realizes the plague was just cover for Count Orlock's killing; however, in light of the film's *cultural context*, *Nosferatu* is an allegory for the Influenza Pandemic itself.

A variety of approaches aid researching the cultural context of silent film. There are published commentaries in books, journals, on distributor websites, or sometimes in Blu-Ray extras or booklets. Even better are period reviews, when they can be located, in academic or online databases (like newspapers .com). Histories of the time period and location (when and where the film was *made*, not set) expose the zeitgeist, fascinations, and concerns that may be reflected in the film. Is the film escapist, allegorical, or clearly referential? What was going on with the director's life or studio finances? What would be on the mind of the audience when they were *not* in the theater?

Exercises or thought experiments

Choose a silent film.

1. Research where it was made; the studio, director, and producers who made it; its stars and other films they appeared in; and how these may have affected how people understood the film.
2. Research its setting – the time and place depicted in the film – and how that setting was understood *at the time of the film's release*. Note perceptions and histories of colonialist locations and depictions of race and gender.

Who needs to prepare, and how much preparation is needed

Everyone needs to prepare, and preparation time is considerable. Even if you are a solo pianist, consider that it will take around five hours just to watch a feature film three times, which is just enough to become familiar with it! You may spend additional time taking notes, preparing a list of scenes, or making an entire *cue list* or *cue sheet* in greater detail.

Once you have written a score, you will need to practice it many times – especially any tricky sections – to make sure you know it and can hit your marks. Memorizing details of the film is necessary for accurate timing, and timing makes the difference between a score that is captivating and one that is phoning it in.

Preparation is particularly important when you have *improvisers* in your performing group. Improvisers, too, have to prepare. If you think someone is just going to improvise on the fly and it's going to be good, it will not. It will be *late*: it will happen after the fact rather than *with the picture*. Improvisers have to *know* what's coming, so they can hit it and be *spot on*.

Anyone who tells you, "Well, I can just show up to the gig and improvise to the film," is doing you a tremendous disservice.

Watching in silence

To better study a film, resist the temptation to watch it with a restored score or someone else's original score. It may ease an initial viewing, but as soon as possible, watch the film with the sound *off*. Not because this replicates silent period viewing – it doesn't; the silent period was filled with sound effects and music – but because it *focuses attention on visual and narrative components*.

Many recorded soundtracks – whether period or contemporary, authentic or irrelevant – obscure the filmmaker's vision and details of the story. It's important to watch the film without auditory distractions, so that you may notice *everything onscreen*. Music *emphasizes certain elements and neglects others* – it may draw your attention to a particular character, but distract you from something else: another character's emotion, the scene's location, or even something happening in the background. You must notice everything, so that you can make your own choices.

Many contemporary scores – even among those accompanying high-end restorations offered on Blu-Ray – tend to bulldoze right through a film, omitting important *sound cues implied by the picture*. These can include background sounds, offscreen sounds, environmental sounds, any number of sounds that might not be as glamorous as a sweeping melody, but that are important for *storytelling*. As discussed below, you can have both: a sweeping melody *and* sounds that bring out these narrative details; these diegetic sounds can be imitated or signaled by music. Watching the film in silence will help you be aware of places where attention to background and offscreen events can help the storytelling.

Watching in silence encourages you to develop *your own ideas*. There are many opportunities and choices to be made: do you hit this character or that character? Do you play a scene with a certain pace or emotion? Do you lead or follow the action? Watching in silence helps you resist the temptation, knowingly or unwittingly, to duplicate approaches in existing scores, approaches that are often not the best anyway!

Repetitive viewing

Noticing everything requires repetitive viewing. At first viewing, many supporting characters may seem indistinguishable, even more so if print quality is poor. Locations may seem ambiguous; props may seem vague or unimportant. The goal of repetitive viewing is to notice *everything* onscreen, to understand *why* things were chosen for inclusion, and to know what they mean.

Subplots

Repetitive viewing brings out *subplots* (consider the old village couple in *Sunrise*) and the *motivation* of supporting roles. Knowing subplots and how minor characters support the story allows a composer to make wise decisions about opportunities for musical emphasis. This knowledge solidifies a *formalist* reading of the film that is highly beneficial for a composer.

The story of Knock in *Nosferatu* is a subplot that adds depth (and comedy) to the film. Knock sends young Hutter off on a fool's errand but meets his own demise in madness. Knock adds mystery to the story: how was he connected with Orlock? How does he understand Orlock's bizarre coded message? Recognizing Knock as a character *with his own storyline* (rather than as just an ancillary supporting character) suggests musical opportunities and interpretations.

Character identities

Repetitive viewing helps you better identify supporting and minor characters. With no audible voices (and inconsistent print quality), filmmakers used a variety of techniques to hammer home character identities. Eventually, you will notice how characters are differentiated through clothing (minor characters may never change outfits); hairstyles, facial hair, makeup, and eyebrows; recurring props; or nervous tics (the pirate always stroking his beard in *The Black Pirate*). Differentiating characters will help you understand a film better, whether or not you give each character a unique theme or musical characterization.

Character arcs

Notice characters who have discernable *character arcs*. Major characters usually learn something or develop in some way over the course of the film. Minor characters can have arcs, too.

In *Nosferatu*, distinguishing Professor Bulwer, Dr. Sievers, and Harding can require multiple viewings; to the casual viewer, they are all just male supporting characters who help push the story forward. Sievers and Harding are not all that interesting, in and of themselves. Professor Bulwer, however, is more interesting because he's in three pivotal scenes.

At the beginning of *Nosferatu*, Bulwer's jovial relationship with Hutter is established. Midway through the film, Bulwer lectures his students about microbes, providing a kind of allegory (or scientific explanation) for the vampire. At the end of *Nosferatu*, Hutter chases after Bulwer for help; in the final scene, Bulwer comes to a realization about what has *really* happened in Wisborg. In fact, Bulwer seems to *bookend* the film, and intertitle cards suggest that the whole story is recounted from his point of view.

Bulwer is a minor role, but even bit characters who show *some* development are more interesting than others who are dramatically static. Bulwer goes from happy innocent to downcast, knowledgeable survivor. Furthermore, he seems to represent *truth* and knowledge acquired through tragedy. While it's not clear he is the narrator, all signs point there.

Locations

Repetitive viewing helps you differentiate locations and the *meaning* behind those locations. The schooner Empusa in *Nosferatu* is a ship, that's clear. Additionally, there is a bifurcation of above deck and below deck. Above deck is open air and represents the known, rational world; below deck is associated with death and mystery. The moment where Orlock ventures above deck is an important transition in his power and menace.

In *Dr. Jekyll and Mr. Hyde*, you should understand how Dr. Jekyll's house, laboratory, and clinic are physically connected, the layout of the physical space within the film world. This becomes important to various entrances and exits, to follow various comings and goings.

In *The Mark of Zorro*, you should understand how Don Diego's house is laid out; this becomes important in the final act, where a secret passage is left open and exposed. In *Nosferatu*, you should be able to distinguish between Hutter's house and Harding's house; this will help you better follow Ellen's storyline.

Note that mastering these details may not be necessary for an *audience* casually watching a film. But for you as a composer, through repetitive viewing, you will better understand the story by grasping all the locations. This can ultimately help the audience if it comes across in your music because you can set things up for them and set the right tone.

Background sounds

We tend to focus on what happens in the foreground: a conversation between main characters, a fight, a chase, or a conflict; but often there are several things going on at once, or there are implied sounds of the *location, weather*, or other *background activity*.

Adding sounds to match these *backgrounds* can make your score more rich and vivid. If you have multiple players, you can spin one off to create these sounds: while one player or players handle a theme or track foreground characters, another player might track something in the background.

Backgrounds can be opportunities for musical sounds, noises, or extended techniques.

Bars and inns are frequent locations in silent films; they appear in *Nosferatu* and *The Phantom Carriage*. Adding sounds of bottles, cups and saucers, or nearby conversations keeps the environment rich and realistic. You can use percussion, key clacks on wind instruments, or even actual murmuring from musicians. The goal is to make the location come alive for the audience.

In big scenes with a large cast, there may be major characters in the foreground, and others in the background. In busy scenes in opera and theatrical productions, directors may give supernumeraries little background dramas to concern themselves with. If there is a scene filled with villagers, pairs of villagers are given things to distract themselves with, arguments to have, and so on. The audience won't be privy to these little dramas, but it makes the scene come alive. Likewise, music can have the same effect following background dramas and situations.

In *Nosferatu*, villagers in the inn are shocked that Hutter wants to go to Orlock's castle – at night no less! While the main drama is between Hutter and the innkeeper, there are other characters in the scene. Their reactions and hubbub, and the *abrupt halt* to their hubbub, are important and can be tracked musically.

The Black Pirate features large, chaotic fight scenes. Douglas Fairbanks is front and center, but there are plenty of his crew and their enemies sword fighting. To make these fights denser, you can have players *track specific pirates*. You'll still get the musical chaos you want, but it will be more enjoyable for players to play and add realism to the fight.

Crowds can be important parts of a story. An angry mob chases Knock in *Nosferatu*. Knock is the foreground character, but the scene benefits from the crowd sounding *alive*. There are moments during the chase when Knock outruns the crowd, and we just see Knock. Do we hear the sound of the angry mob in the distance? Do we hear them offscreen? Do we keep the sound of the crowd alive during the entire sequence?

Agitated countryfolk, their lanterns casting flickering shadows, rush to the docks in *Sunrise*; their commotion wakes up the sleeping City Woman. Do we hear the crowd outside her room *before* she wakes up?

In these and other cases, background sounds have narrative importance, and can provide inspiration for composing an effective musical score.

Environmental sounds

Filling in environmental sounds makes an original score richer and thicker. Environmental sounds can be sounds of nature, but also sounds of street traffic (*Sunrise*), the hubbub of a crowd (*Nosferatu*), mechanical sounds (*Metropolis*), or anything that fills out the environmental setting of a film.

Consider your film 53

These sounds can be created subtly, and can employ creative and extended techniques.

Ellen is deep in thought on a desolate beach in *Nosferatu*. What does it sound like? Is there wind, or surf? Colored noise or various blown textures on wind instruments work well for these sounds. Sometimes a recorder or alto flute works better than a standard flute in C. Sometimes a clarinet or saxophone mouthpiece works well on its own. On string instruments, bowing *sul ponticello* (near the bridge) or playing harmonics can yield nice effects. Portamento harmonics played *sul ponticello* can give an effect sounding like the crying of seagulls.

Seafaring ships ply the open sea in *The Black Pirate* and *Nosferatu*. Do the ships groan and creak? Creak tone (bowing slow and heavy on the string) on double bass is good for this, and for implying the sounds of deep waves, raising and lowering the bow of the ship.

Even if you're composing a relatively straightforward tonal score, environmental sounds offer you the opportunity to expand your palette with contemporary effects and extended techniques. This can help push your score into a more exciting contemporary musical space.

Exercises or thought experiments

It is possible to play back prerecorded sounds or samples in live performance. Do you think this is a desirable approach? When is this useful? When should it be avoided?

Oarsmen transport Orlock's coffins downriver on a raft in *Nosferatu*. How can you create the rush and gurgle of the river?

Towards the end of *Sunrise*, the village comes alive with urgent activity, waking up the City Woman. How can you create sounds of agitated villagers?

Machines permeate the dystopian environment of *Metropolis*. How might you create these machine sounds?

How might alternate and surreal realities be presented in *The Phantom Carriage*? What kinds of environmental sounds would they have?

Offscreen sounds

Watching a film with the sound *off*, you will discover instances where characters *react to offscreen sound* even *before* you see its diegetic source. While this is common in sound film, many people don't realize it happens in silent film, too!

These instances are important to notice because they provide a visual cue that you have an opportunity to *track offscreen sound*. The benefit of tracking offscreen sound is that the movie comes to life and makes more logical sense. Here are some examples of implied or obvious offscreen sounds.

In *Nosferatu*, Orlock and Hutter, in their first meeting in Orlock's castle, react to the clock striking midnight, *before* the picture cuts to the clock (ca. 00:24:30). Ideally, you could add a chiming sound that starts just *before* their reaction shots, so that we hear the chime, see their reactions, and then see the clock. We would say this chime sound *prelaps* the shot of the clock.

A viewer might miss this moment when watching a DVD or Blu-Ray with a restored or original score where *prelapped* chimes are left out (simply coinciding with the shot of the clock), or the chimes are not hit at all. Prelapping the shot of the clock with chimes is beneficial: the reaction shots make more sense, and the viewing experience is more logical.

In *Sunrise*, there's a moment where The Man decides *not* to kill his Wife, and throws up his arms, covering his face in shame or revulsion (ca. 00:31:00). He begins rowing their rowboat furiously, and we see a long shot of the village church. There is an opportunity here to add distant church bells ringing *just before* he throws his arms up; this would imply a logical reason for his sudden change of heart. If the score fails to emphasize that we see a *church* from *his point of view*, the scene still works but makes less sense. Having a church bell *prelap* his decision *not* to kill his Wife makes the scene more logical.

In *Sunrise*, lantern light splashes around the City Woman's room, suggesting offscreen commotion, which wakes her (ca. 01:20:25). We see the dancing lantern light *before* we see the agitated villagers; it would make sense to have sound or music similarly track the offscreen commotion.

Offscreen sounds are not just prelaps, but moments where we might keep a plot point alive, *prolonging* its presence through sound or music. Offscreen sound can accentuate what characters are hearing. There is a sequence with a runaway piglet in *Sunrise* (ca. 01:00:50); even when the pig is not onscreen, we might *still* hear it squealing. In *Sunrise*, a runaway dog breaks from its chain (ca. 00:25:40); we might still hear it yapping even offscreen.

Offscreen sounds provide us with choices, decisions, and opportunities. We should watch a film enough to spot occasions where offscreen sounds or music might be part of our score.

Spotting: choosing which moments to play

Choosing what to play or hit, deciding where music comes in and out, is called *spotting* the film. In a silent film score, you may want music more or less throughout the film; this is likely to be the case, except for dramatic pauses or major structural separations (such as the beginning and endings of acts, as in *Nosferatu*).

Still, spotting questions remain: given multiple possibilities, what do you want music to accomplish? How do you want scenes to be paced? What kind of tension and release, climaxes, resolutions, and relaxations should the music attain? How are these timed? Such planning is part of spotting. These decisions can be documented in *spotting notes*.

You may want to write down a list of *cues* to help you with spotting; the cues in this list may be musical or visual. Some of this terminology is a bit slippery. You may be familiar with a "cue" as a signal to a theatrical actor, or as a neighboring part indicated in an orchestral musician's own part that prepares their entrance. A *cue*, in contemporary film music, is a piece of music in a film; or, it can refer abstractly to the *place in a film* where a piece of music *will go*, as delimited by start and stop points. A director might give a composer a list of cues they would like to have written.

Cue lists, cue sheets, and spotting notes

We benefit from some semantic clarification. Some people might call this list of cues a *cue sheet*, but this term has some specific meanings within specific time periods.

In the *silent period*, a studio might send out a *cue sheet* comprising notated or suggested musical selections for an accompanist to play for a particular picture. Musicologists and performers reconstructing period scores are particularly interested in these historic cue sheets.[9]

In *contemporary media scoring* and film music business, a *cue sheet* may refer to detailed, standardized documentation of every piece of music in a film: an identifying number (1M01, 1M02), its name, exact timing, usage, authors, publishers, and percentages of ownership. Film producers will file this document with relevant performing rights organizations (like ASCAP and BMI) to ensure accurate payment of performance royalties to composers and publishers.

Today, post-production sound crews might have a simplified continuity sheet or list of scenes that helps a music editor take *spotting notes* in a music spotting meeting with a composer and director. (Sound effects might have their own spotting meeting.) These spotting notes contain ideas and suggestions for the music.

For our purposes, we might want an exhaustive list of potential cues or screen action that may cue or inform our music. This *cue list* – whether it's proposed musical pieces or onscreen events – can be cursory or can go into great detail. You might just want a simple ordered list of musical selections; that suffices for planning mood music for many films. An action film might demand greater detail. The more dynamic and reactive your score, the greater detail you may require.

The draft cue list shown in Figure 2.1 documents about two minutes of screen time in *The Mark of Zorro*. Consulting this list, you can visualize significant onscreen events and get a sense of timing. Locations are noted ("Int. Stable") as well as angles where helpful ("Wide shot: Bernardo sleeping at desk"). Timings are notated in places to help correlate the cue list with a video file; you can include timings in as much detail as you find helpful.

56 Consider your film

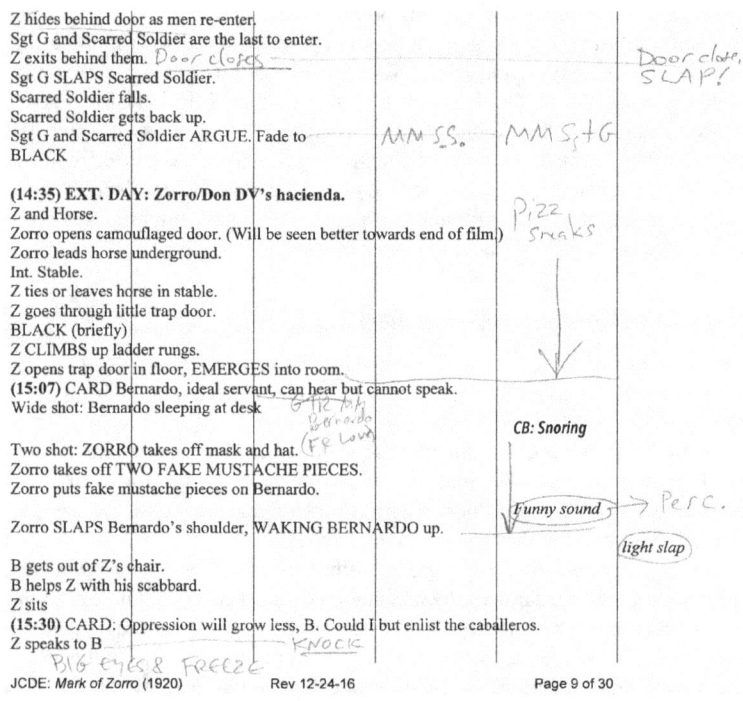

Figure 2.1 Draft cue list for *The Mark of Zorro*. © 2016 Jack Curtis Dubowsky.

A cue list can form the foundation for an ensuing musical score. Notice the pencil annotations in Figure 2.1. Already elements of the score are being sketched: percussion hits, pizzicato sneaks, and *mickey-mousing* ("MM") dialogue between characters. (These techniques are discussed further in Chapters 3 and 4.) This cue list shows how the scoring process begins by studying the film, noting cinematic and narrative events. When those are laid upon the page, you have a formula that can structure your score. The cue list (and your score) can evolve as needed. The more carefully you study and know your film, the better your score will be.

Figure 2.2 shows the corresponding section of *The Mark of Zorro* from the finished cue book. (*Themes and cue book* notation is discussed in Chapter 4.) Cues have been revised and abbreviated; each lane refers to an instrument; the boxes show when and what they play. The cue list was a preliminary step toward this finished score.

You may notice the "Fade to: BLACK" that separates two scenes. While the music seems to end and begin anew with the second scene, this isn't

Consider your film   57

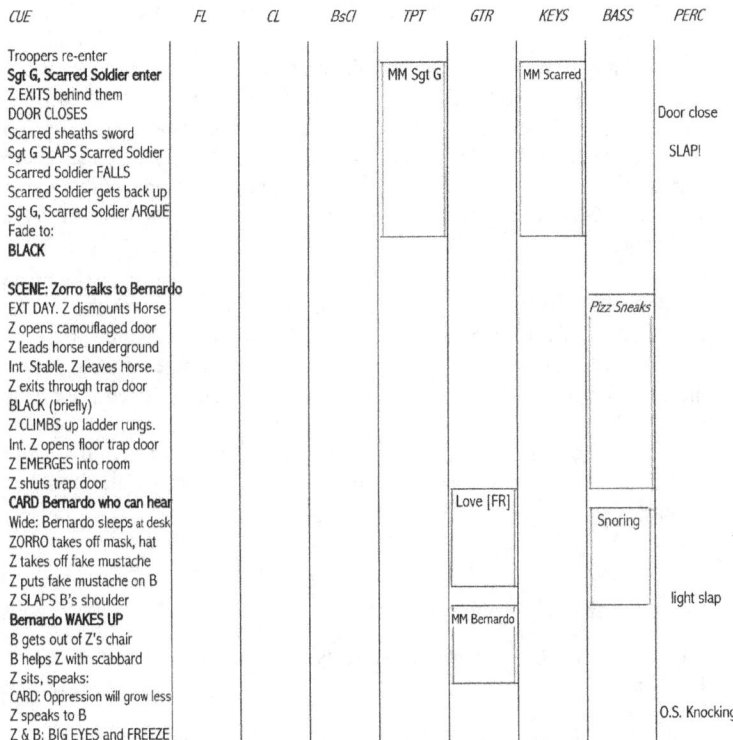

Figure 2.2 Cue book for *The Mark of Zorro* live score © 2017 Jack Curtis Dubowsky / De Stijl Music.

always the best approach. The mickey-mousing could extend over the black, or the pizzicato sneaks could *prelap* the new scene. Or, you could have both, and they could overlap. Any of these approaches can be cued by a conductor in performance, but a desired option could be written right into the cue book.

Scene divisions

It might feel natural to have music start and end with each scene (or even each *reel* – a method harkening to *apparatus theory*). This, however, is a poor and uninteresting approach, especially if overused. Having music track scenes start-to-finish was seen as artless and lazy even during the Nickelodeon period. In 1911, "Our Music Page" in *The Moving Picture News* bemoaned,

The average musician is under the impression that it is necessary for them to change the music with each scene as it occurs in the picture – but this idea is entirely wrong; it would do more harm than good [...] Good judgment must be used in dividing the picture so as to pick out the important situations and to select the main theme of the subject to be played for – you must make it a point to try and play the pictures just as smooth as you can, and try and avoid that undesirable break, that so often is heard, and that is entirely uncalled for. [Good music] cannot be produced by trying to follow each and every scene and insert music to fit the individual scene as it appears.[10]

Music divisions should not necessarily match scene divisions; this is the approach of an "average musician." The film should be spotted to "pick out the important situations," and to prioritize those moments. Transitions should be planned to avoid the "undesirable break" and to keep the music "smooth" while it supports the film. Music can serve to bridge transitions and scene changes, making a film more fluid. Music can lead us into and out of scenes, and music can itself break or transition at appropriate moments mid-scene.

Exercises or thought experiments

Choose a silent short, or one to two reels of a feature silent film, about 10–20 minutes.

1. Create a *cue list*: a sequential list of shots and onscreen action. Use very short descriptions.

How much detail do you want or need in this list? Does it give you some spotting ideas? Can you use it as the basis for musical spotting notes?

Choose a silent short, or one to two reels of a feature silent film, about 10–20 minutes.

1. Write down some *spotting notes*, where you'd want music, and what music would do.
2. Write down a second set of spotting notes, imagining different approaches.
3. Write some simple music, a rough draft, to test your spotting notes. See how well each approach works.
4. How does creating spotting notes in advance shape your composition?

Tentpoles: important sequences

These "important situations," sometimes called "tentpole scenes,"[11] are moments critical to the film; they should be handled delicately. Tentpoles aren't unique to silent film, and they aren't necessarily big action scenes. Narratively, tentpoles can be major turning points that help define the story.

Sunrise has two mirrored, pivotal moments: first, from The Wife, second, from The Man. The Wife, briefly left alone in a little rowboat, realizes a dangerous character flaw in her husband (ca. 00:27:20). Without dialogue (or intertitles), actor Janet Gaynor slowly reveals her dark realization; it directly causes her flight to The City. Her epiphany in the rowboat is an opportunity for music to help show her thoughts – although you don't want to overplay the scene and ruin its delicacy.[12]

Later, The Man cries for forgiveness in the city cathedral (ca. 00:42:00). His repentance directly causes a transformation in their relationship that is exploited in the ensuing act. The film *depends* on these tentpole scenes to succeed, or none of the ensuing action makes any sense. The film has other pivotal moments as well, but these hold up the film in their temporal vicinity.

One approach to composing a film score is to identify and score tentpole scenes *first*; this can solidify your approach to the whole film. If the tentpoles are working, the rest becomes easier to fill in.

Exercises or thought experiments

Choose a feature length silent film.

1. Identify three to five tentpole scenes or sequences.
2. What makes them tentpoles?
3. How would you handle them musically?

Budgeting and rights

In considering your film, another area to address is expenses related to the film itself, and how and where you plan to present it.

If a film is slated for *public* screening, you must account for the cost of the film's rental fees or performance license. While the original film as IP (*intellectual property*) may have fallen into the public domain – its *characters* and *story* may be re-used and appropriated freely – theatrical rights may *not* be public domain. This is certainly the case with *restorations*, which are the property of the company that invested in the restoration. Hypothetically, if you have your very own 1920 print of a Fox Pictures film, you may be able to screen that with impunity. However, if you are grabbing a copy from a DVD, it's likely you need to pay a rental fee to a company that holds theatrical rights. Distributors have leverage over theaters: if they are not paid, they can withhold other films from their catalog from a theater.

Depending on your location, presenter, and venue, it may make sense to have the presenter or venue handle booking the print, especially if they have an established relationship with the distributor. If you are arranging a screening at a university, some distributors have special arrangements and contacts.[13] Established relationships and expertise can help in negotiating with a distributor. The executive director of a non-profit, arthouse cinema in California explains in detail,

> It is strongly advisable for musicians to lean on their host cinema to leverage their established relationships with their studios in negotiating exhibition fees for their titles. When a musician reaches out directly to a distributor, they will more than likely be handed their standard exhibition fee; moreover, as a new client, a musician will almost always have to create a new credit account with a distributor, which involves a ton of paperwork and often even credit checks, before they can obtain exhibition rights to a title. A cinema, on the other hand, has a business history with their distributors, and can often negotiate concessions in pricing when working with their representative based on the nature of the event. For example, by letting their representative know that the theater will also be incurring a musician's fee for the live-score, a distributor may offer a reduced "flat fee," as opposed to the more traditional fee of a percentage of tickets sold, in consideration of that added expense. Or if a particular distributor doesn't bend on percentage-based fees, the theater may be able to negotiate a percentage based on their standard ticket fee – for example, if the theater generally charges $10 for a film ticket, but the live-score event is priced at the higher rate of $35 based on the additional expense of the musicians, a theater can explain this to a distributor, who is already familiar with their traditional $10 ticket fee, and the distributor may agree to charge a percentage of ticket sales based on a ticket price of $10 per seat, and not the full price of $35. In short, it is common for distributors to consider the specifics of a particular event when determining their exhibition fee – but they're not going to do so for a new client. When producing a live-score event in a movie theater, have the theater book the title.[14]

Partnering with an established venue or presenter has other benefits as well: the venue may have its own social media following, email lists, and local following, and these will boost ticket sales.

Other costs for presenting a live score event include publicity, advertising, hiring musicians, renting rehearsal space, flyering, social media expenses, cartage, and so on. Typically, that's on you, not the presenter or the venue (although they may promote the show in their own social media accounts and monthly calendars). In addition to money, a great amount of time is invested as well. For some presenters, a live score event can be daunting logistically. Other presenters find (or can be convinced) that it will bring cachet to their venue. Says the Board Chair of another non-profit art house cinema:

> The process of bringing unique, limited run content to a theatre audience can be extremely challenging. The costs of pre-production to the artist, advertising, promotion, licensing and distribution can easily overwhelm ticket sales. But the experience can be magical, so the effort needs to be made.[15]

It makes sense to draw up a budget for a live score event. Ticket sales are not easy to predict in advance. You may, however, be okay with operating at a loss, for the experience, or to establish your name, or build your reputation. Drawing up a budget will help you ascertain how much money you can afford to spend on your players: how many musicians you can afford to hire, how much you can afford to pay them each, and how many "services"[16] or rehearsals you can afford. The choice of players is discussed in the next chapter, "Consider your score."

Notes

1 Saunders, Alfred H., Editor. (1911). "Our Music Column." *The Moving Picture News*. Vol. IV, No. 25. June 24, 1911. p. 9. (New York: The Cinematograph Publishing Company).
2 Christie, Ian. (2000). "Formalism and Neo-Formalism" in *Film Studies: Critical Approaches*. Edited by John Hill and Pamela Church Gibson. (New York: Oxford University Press). p. 56.
3 Ibid., p. 56.
4 Ibid., pp. 57–8.
5 For additional discussion see Goldmark, Daniel. (2005). *Tunes for 'Toons*. (Berkeley, CA: University of California Press). pp. 15–16.
6 Saunders, Alfred H., Editor. (1911). "Our Music Column." *The Moving Picture News*. Vol. IV, No. 25. June 24, 1911. p. 9. (New York: The Cinematograph Publishing Company).
7 "There is one thing that the musician must at all times strive to do, that is, get into the spirit of the picture, allow yourself as much as possible to become enveloped in the atmosphere that you think the producer was trying to accomplish, bring out each and every point as clear and distinct as possible. If the picture is a comedy, help it along and thus help carry out the idea the producer had in mind. A drama may have both serious and comic elements in its make-up; very often in a dramatic picture it is possible to introduce a laugh where none was intended, and this you must be very careful to avoid at all times as it is very liable to interfere with a serious or important scene, for there is always some ass in the average audience who will laugh at anything, at any time." Saunders, Alfred H., Editor. (1911). "Our Music Column." *The Moving Picture News*. Vo. IV, No. 46. November 18, 1911. p. 36. (New York: The Cinematograph Publishing Company).

8 "Gradually, musical cliches [sic], tags, and popular songs became unfashionable. With the advent of the feature-length photoplay, the picture palace and more refined musical accompaniments, cliches [sic] and 'old favorites' (like sound effects) were relegated to serving comedy where 'funning the film' was deemed acceptable." Berg, Charles Merrell. (1973). *An Investigation of the Motives for and Realization of Music to Accompany the American Silent Film, 1896–1927*. p. 199 (Dissertation). University of Iowa.
9 As of this writing, some silent period cue sheets can be found online at the Silent Film Sound & Music Archive, https://www.sfsma.org/ARK/22915/category/cue-sheets/
10 Saunders, Alfred H., Editor. (1911). "Our Music Page." *The Moving Picture News*. Vol. IV, Np. 29. July 22, 1911. p. 9. (New York: The Cinematograph Publishing Company).
11 Dubowsky, Jack C. (2011). "The Evolving 'Temp Score' in Animation" in *Music, Sound, and the Moving Image*. Vol. 5, Issue 1. Spring 2011. p. 6. (Liverpool: Liverpool University Press).
12 In contrast, I would argue that the chase that *follows* The Wife's realization (ca. 00:32:10) is a good example of an action sequence that is *not* a tentpole, being a bit of a throwaway sequence that serves primarily to transport the couple into The City.
13 See https://www.kinolorberedu.com for example.
14 Crow, Logan. (2022). Executive Director and Founder, The Frida Cinema, Santa Ana, California. Email to author, June 20, 2022.
15 Van Dijs, Jan. (2022). Board Chair, Art Theater of Long Beach. Email to author, June 11, 2022.
16 "Services" refers to both rehearsals *and* performances; basically, anytime a musician has to show up. Many professional musicians may not care to distinguish between a rehearsal and a performance, it's their *time* they are selling, so the number of services includes all rehearsals and performances.

Bibliography

Berg, Charles Merrell. (1973). *An Investigation of the Motives of and Realization of Music to Accompany the American Silent Film, 1896-1927* (Dissertation). (University of Iowa), p. 199.

Christie, Ian. (2000). "Formalism and Neo-Formalism." In *Film Studies: Critical Approaches*. Edited by Hill, John and Gibson, Pamela Church (New York: Oxford University Press).

Goldmark, Daniel. (2005). *Tunes For 'Toons* (Berkeley: University of California Press), pp. 15–16.

Saunders, Alfred H., Editor. (1911, June 24). "Our Music Column." *The Moving Picture News*, Vol. IV, No. 25 (New York: The Cinematograph Publishing Company), p. 9.

Saunders, Alfred H., Editor. (1911, November 18). "Our Music Column." *The Moving Picture News*, Vol. IV, No. 46 (New York: The Cinematograph Publishing Company), p. 36.

3 Consider your score

This chapter helps composers look ahead and make thoughtful decisions in planning a score. We look at musical concerns including planning themes, choice of ensemble, as well as aesthetic and compositional choices. This chapter helps composers consider musical opportunities presented in silent film, in particular how music can be placed, and how music can work with common cinematic tropes. While contemporary sound films have similar (or identical) concerns, silent films broaden our possibilities *musically*, even as they demand special care to remain faithful to a film *dramatically*, whose writer, director, and creative team are long gone.

Plan your themes

Strong themes give a score its own identity; in many cases, films become inseparable from their musical themes: *Star Wars*, *The Godfather*, *Jaws*, and *Psycho*, to name a few. Composers enjoy and take pride in writing memorable themes.

Themes are best deployed *strategically*. It's wise to plot major themes in advance: what they might represent, where they should be prominent or fully stated, and where they should be used with restraint or in *development*, or quoted in a *fragment*.

When *characters* have their own recognizable themes, this helps audiences identify them. Strong themes lend themselves to many variations: changing modality can make them happy, sad, or otherwise shift their mood; changes in meter, rhythm, and tempo can create or moderate energy and excitement. Variations are helpful when characters undergo transformation or changing circumstance.

Themes do not need to be tied to characters, however. Themes connected to *abstract concepts* can be equally effective: themes for home, loss, death, happiness, truth, war, or madness, for instance. Themes can be tied to *location*: the village, the city, the ocean; *Metropolis* has the city in the air, the city underground, and the catacombs – these could be treated with different themes, tonalities, or orchestral colors.

64 Consider your score

Planning musical themes and tying them to story or cinematic elements help a composer sketch an overview of the score. *Naming* these themes and plotting their use in the film – *before even composing them* – lends organization and a solid framework to the score and the composition process.

Exercises or thought experiments

Choose a feature-length silent film to watch in its entirety.

1. *Without composing any music*, plan themes you'd want to have for the film. How many would there be? What would they represent? What would you call them? How often would they occur? How could they develop? Would they lend themselves to any particular variations?
2. Name these themes.

Sketch your themes

Once you have ideas for what themes you need – or even just a feel for a film – you can start improvising to the film. Your goal is to come up with some musical ideas that connect with the themes you have already planned and named. Don't be critical about what you play; try different approaches. Try playing outside of stock-in-trade chord progressions, patterns, or idioms to which you are accustomed. Stretch yourself while seeing *what fits the picture*. Write down (or record) anything that seems like it has potential, so you don't forget it.

With a clear sense of the themes you have planned and named, you can compose thematic ideas *without* running the film. This gives you extra creative freedom, being able to sit with your favorite instrument or with manuscript paper, and, knowing you need a theme for, say, victory, or sadness, or a particular character, just focus on writing music. If you have studied your film, you don't need to watch it to write music.

You can compose music *before* you have determined the forces of the performing ensemble. You can compose music in *reduction* or *short score* in advance, working and fleshing out musical ideas. You might compose in your head, at the piano, on the guitar, or on a computer – but a short score of two to four staves is a clear, flexible way to jot down ideas and perfect them. You can subsequently arrange this music for *any* ensemble. Ideally, one might plan *beforehand* the most fitting (or likely) ensemble to perform the score. This isn't strictly necessary, even if there are benefits to knowing what instruments you are likely to have at your disposal.

Consider your score 65

Figure 3.1 Short score sketch from *Dr. Jekyll and Mr. Hyde*, © 2018 Jack Curtis Dubowsky / De Stijl Music.

Themes do not need to be tonal. They can relate to register, brightness, density, or rhythm. Rather than being a *melody*, a theme could be a rumbling, a chirping, a *pitch set*, or a *melodic contour*. For contemporary audiences, "silent film" inhabits an "art house" space, and an experimental score is more welcome here than in a sound film where it would fight a dialogue track. This freedom from a dialogue track allows (and even encourages you) to take musical risks, to exploit volume, loudness, color, and opportunities that would be rejected by the director of a sound film. Make good use of this freedom.

It's wise to consider how themes *develop*. Are they fully stated from the get-go, or do they begin as a *fragment* that builds throughout the film until revealed in full length and majesty at a climactic moment? Are themes constructed so they can *interact* musically? Can two themes be played simultaneously thanks to careful counterpoint?

Above is an example of a sketch in short score (Figure 3.1). It shows a high part, chords, and an independent bassline in three staves.

While the high part's pedal tone is not complex, separating it on its own staff differentiates it clearly. Similarly, having the bass part explicitly notated emphasizes its importance. The syncopated middle line is given in *both* chord chart and note notation; this could be played exactly as written or *comped* by rhythm instruments. (Chapter 4 shows a short score supplied as final notation for players.)

Exercises or thought experiments

1. Using one (or more) of the named themes from the previous exercise, compose some music *without running the film*.
2. Using the film chosen in the earlier exercise, run the film and improvise to it freely, keeping in mind the themes you thought to develop.

3. Sketch a theme that is non-tonal. Sketch a theme that is microtonal. Sketch a theme that is rhythmic or has no pitch component whatsoever.
4. Compose two themes that can be played simultaneously. Can you make them different moods? Can you make them different tempos? Can you make them different meters? Can they have different tonal centers or modes? What is the effect of combining them?
5. Using the film chosen in the earlier exercise, compose the named themes, either for lead sheet or piano.
6. Compose variations of the themes.

Choice of ensemble

In *artistic* terms, choice of ensemble involves what instruments might best communicate your score. For *The Mark of Zorro*, guitar, mandolin, or bandurria might evoke colonial Spanish California. Action adventures might benefit from percussion.

Sometimes instruments appear onscreen, suggesting their inclusion. A guitar appears in *The Phantom Carriage*; a piano appears in *Dr. Jekyll and Mr. Hyde*. Bassoons and a shofar appear onscreen in *The Golem*. A dance band, brass instruments, and a bell carillon appear in *Sunrise*. Being able to include the sounds of onscreen instruments in your score helps tie it to the film.

In *practical* terms, to choose the forces of an ensemble, one must know the budget; venue size; number or specialties of players demanded (do players double?); and the number of rehearsals needed or possible. A large venue may *require* more players (or even amplification) to fill the room with sound; a small house may only have physical space for a handful of players at most. Budgetary restrictions will limit your choice of players, of course; this is an obvious caveat to the information that follows.

Instrument characteristics and combinations

When planning the ensemble, a composer might consider characteristics of the film at hand. Swashbucklers like *The Mark of Zorro* or *The Black Pirate* may benefit from clangy percussion. *Onscreen appearances* may encourage specific instruments: the Salvation Army singer's guitar in *The Phantom Carriage*, or the shofar in *The Golem*. Some films may suggest specific styles based on their *setting*, like colonial Spanish California in *The Mark of Zorro*.

Silent films were often performed with specialized *sound effects*, a continuation from vaudeville and theater.[1] Percussionists can carry this role musically. Keyboardists can play back prerecorded samples, loops, and ambiences if desired. Any instrument may have its own idiomatic sounds or noises: tapping the body of a double bass makes a convincing door knock; col legno tapping effects can imitate insects or vermin; wind instruments are good for a variety of airy effects. The needs of the film may imply a choice of instruments.

You might *first* decide what instruments you *require*, then prioritize others that can contribute to the widest array of situations, such as piano or double bass. It's helpful to find players who *double* on a number of instruments: many flute players play piccolo or alto flute, and many reed players play clarinet, bass clarinet, and saxophone. Many musicians, no matter their primary instrument, can play some acoustic guitar, banjo, hand percussion, or recorder. You cannot rely on this, however; you need to ask. Players who double on multiple instruments are highly desirable for silent film ensembles.

Some instruments have multiple registers or playing techniques that provide different characteristics, so they may be suitable for multiple roles in *mickey-mousing* or character interpretations. (See Chapter 4 for more on mickey-mousing.) All clarinets have a high, piercing *clarino* register, and a low, rich *chalumeau* register. An instrument like this can take on two roles, and keep them differentiated. String instruments offer arco (bowed) or pizzicato techniques that are distinct and distinguishable by any audience member.

Where you have opposing roles, such as hero and villain, or roles that appear in many scenes *together* – such as hero and love interest – you might choose two different instruments that provide contrasting sounds throughout the film. When assigning instruments their roles or functions in a score, consider screen time, characterization, instrument register, tonal characteristics, beneficial pairings, and so on.

In a way, you are casting instruments analogous to the way a director might cast actors in a film. Additionally, you have technical considerations; while every instrument deserves a rest, a wind or brass instrument simply cannot play nonstop throughout a feature film in the same way a keyboard can.

Exercises or thought experiments

Choose a silent feature film; identify the main characters.

1. Imagine you have a guitar, a double bass, a keyboard, a flute, a clarinet, and a saxophone. If you wanted to assign an instrument to each main character, how would you do it? Upon what factors or ideas would you base your decision?
2. Imagine you could have any instruments you like. What instruments would best suit those characters, and why?

> 3. Repeat this exercise using different films and different combinations of instruments. What would you do if you had a woodwind quintet? What would you do with a small jazz combo? What would you do with a string quartet or a percussion ensemble?

Solo piano

Solo piano's long tradition of silent film accompaniment dates back to the Lumière brothers' public demonstrations and to storefront nickelodeons, well before the opulent movie palaces of the 1920s were built. These early pianists laid a groundwork of harmonic and rhythmic clichés pulled from popular song and light opera.

The piano, of course, is capable of much more than this preliminary vocabulary of clichés. By 1933, Kurt London, an inceptive critic and historian of film music, bemoaned the "beginning of the pianist period" in early cinema:

> At the outset, his repertoire remained a matter of complete indifference; he played anything he liked, and there was little or no connection between music and the film it accompanied.[2]

This indifferent repertoire, of course, would change, as film accompanists became more sophisticated. Nevertheless, today, over one hundred years after this "pianist period," audiences still harbor expectations of silent film music: a theater organ or an out of tune piano mining stock gestures from compiler Ernö Rapée.[3] A video of "John Williams Plays the silent era (featuring John Williams on Piano)" exemplifies these gestures; this performance is often regarded as *satire*.[4]

While it requires skill and practice to convincingly emulate this style, you do *not* have to abide by or regurgitate these expected clichés. I would ask you *not* to. Ideally, you are on a journey finding your own voice as a pianist, improviser, and composer. Composing for silent film is an ideal path for this journey; you should take advantage of the freedom to explore, experiment, and improvise. The goal is not to imitate a perceived silent style, but, in the words of Kurt London, to emphasize the "connection between music and the film." This can be done in as contemporary or abstract a manner as you wish. Paul Bley, Keith Jarrett, and Cecil Taylor took the piano in new directions, and you can too. For a guide to extended techniques, see Alan Shockley's *The Contemporary Piano: A Performer and Composer's Guide to Techniques and Resources* (2018).

Exploitable characteristics of the piano include its large range and potential as a percussion instrument. You may think about differentiating characters rhythmically or in terms of *register*; where on the keyboard do they live? You can expand the piano's sound palette with extended techniques like strumming bare strings; hitting, slapping, or knocking parts of the instrument; holding the pedal while screaming or making sounds into the case to vibrate the strings; or using *prepared piano*.

Accompanying a feature film on solo piano can be a lot of work; the whole score rests on your shoulders alone. Planning should be made so you don't wear yourself out, find yourself in spots where you don't know what to do, or go into automatic mode, playing on autopilot.

Many pianists and composers rely heavily on *ostinatos* and arpeggios to fill space or take time, creating a fabric from *muscle memory* that keeps music going but allows them to take a mental break. While ostinatos and arpeggios can be useful and mesmerizing, one should take care that they do not become a crutch in creating music for silent film. Can you fill space other than with repeating figuration?

Compositional techniques, discussed in other books and in your private lessons, can help you immensely. If melody repeats, can rhythm be varied? Can you use rhythmic augmentation or diminution? If rhythm repeats, can pitches vary? Can expression change? Can you reharmonize melodies or change modality? Can you invert themes, reverse them, or develop their melodic contour? Improvisation skills help tremendously, but that does *not* mean just playing arbitrary stuff. Ideally, you should build your musical prowess so you can develop and adapt your themes and existing material on the fly.

Exercises or thought experiments

Improvisation exercises for piano.

1. Play something entirely rhythmic and non-legato. Do not use the pedal. Use the piano entirely as a percussive instrument. Try different meters, rhythms, and tempos.
2. Contrast that with another section that is legato.
3. Make a character sketch using only the very low notes of the piano.
4. Make a character sketch that uses only the high notes of the piano.
5. Choose (or compose) a very simple theme or melody and, continuing to play very simply, see how many ways you can vary or manipulate it. Avoiding unnecessary virtuosity, playing well within your abilities, see how you can twist it and reshape it.

Theater organ

Theater organ (or cinema organ) has its own storied history; it developed from church and cathedral organs, with an eye towards dramatically expanding the sound palette available for film accompaniment, even including percussion instruments.[5] The instrument became associated with cinema, widely installed in opulent movie palaces in the 1920s.

Organ performance is a specialized area; organs and keyboards may be playable by a pianist, but they have their own idiosyncrasies and performance techniques. Organs may have a pedal board, volume swell pedals, intricate stops and settings, and so on.

A notable characteristic of the organ is its ability to *sustain*. Unlike a piano, whose notes decay immediately after being struck, the organ better imitates acoustic instruments and legato passages. Like the piano, the organ has its own set of clichés, and has the same issue for a single player to remain attentive and focused throughout a feature-length performance.

A contemporary organist might consider changing stops or twiddling knobs *while* playing a sound, as opposed to just changing presets. The ability for low tones to vibrate the whole theater can be exploited for its own effect, creating a kind of Sensurround. The use of atonality will further pull the organ away from its existing clichés. I advocate for the organist to expand the way the instrument is used, rather than just fulfilling audience expectations.

The electronic musician

A contemporary version of the cinema organist (and one with a more portable setup) could be a synthesizer player. A further extension of this is the *electronic musician*, who might have any number of setups, instruments, effects, compositional approaches, and performance modalities.

This book encourages you to think of the electronic musician broadly: they could be a programmer or an instrument builder. They might use any kind of control surface or computer device, not necessarily a keyboard. They might work alone, or in a group, like the Edison Studio collective from Italy, who specialize in electroacoustic scores for silent film.[6]

Electronic musicians have a number of possibilities of things they can do, things they excel at, things they can add or bring to the table. The possibilities are nearly endless, but can be thought of in three broad categories: triggering samples, live processing, and synthesis or sound design.

Triggering samples – using any control surface or device – plays back prerecorded sounds. These can range from one-shot hits to long ambiences. They can be melodic or percussive. Using an unusual or custom-made control surface can suggest new approaches or look intriguing to an audience.

Live processing allows a performer to take sounds, acoustic or electronic, performed by themselves or by others, and in real time, using effects or computers, alter those sounds. This technique has powerful possibilities for live scores. We can imagine chases where a beat is manipulated or filtered to match approach and escape, proximity and distance. We can imagine character themes that are distorted or bitcrushed if a character becomes unsettled or angry. Live processing adds another layer to sound and meaning, and can be used collaboratively with multiple players, where the electronic musician manipulates miked acoustic sounds.[7]

Electronic musicians may specialize in synthesis or sound design. They may use modular synthesizers or build homemade instruments. Examples of builder-performers include Mark Applebaum, an electroacoustic composer, improviser, and instrument builder, and British electronic musician and instrument builder Sam Battles, who works under the name Look Mum No Computer.[8] Building can involve everything from circuit bending – altering old electronic devices to make new sounds – to making inventive control or input devices, to building or programming complex systems from scratch. The exciting possibility here is that with the time and energy, an instrument builder might make something specifically designed for the needs of a chosen film.

The electronic musician could be one member of a larger group, and might play an acoustic instrument as well; some techniques like *looping* have become popular among musicians of all kinds. If an electronic musician performs a live score on their own, they still have a vast array of capabilities that can vary their score. They might incorporate the possibilities of *generative music*, or music that self-generates based upon existing parameters, to give themselves moments to relax a bit during a long film, or to supply a texture that evolves and continues on its own while they add other sounds.

Duet

Performing a live score as a duet starts to add possibilities as well as relief during a long film, where two players can trade off duties. Having multi-instrumentalists is a benefit, with the creation of a variety of sounds possible. While some duets, like piano and percussion, might imply a straightforward approach, you can do interesting things with an unusual duet. A bassoon and a banjo might challenge you to explore extended techniques or unusual approaches. There is really no combination that would not work; there are challenges to any duet, and there are benefits to choosing contrasting instruments.

Small ensemble

Three to four players can be considered a small ensemble for the purposes of live score to silent film. Alloy Orchestra was just three players, and built a strong national reputation. It's easier to tour, and to take shows to distant venues, with a small ensemble than with a large one.

Small ensembles have other benefits: you don't need a conductor; musicians can play off each other with ease; players can rest while another takes a scene; you have a variety of different possible combinations. Arranging music for small ensemble, you can start to think in terms of solos, duets, and tuttis.

72 Consider your score

With three to four players, you open up a broader palette of sounds and the ability to track multiple things: one player might play a theme; one or two players might mickey-mouse or improvise onscreen characters; one player might handle environmental sounds or ambience. Scores begin to offer more depth and complexity with just three to four players.

Midsize ensemble

Five to eight players can be considered a midsize ensemble. With this number of players, it can help to add a conductor, or have a player who can conduct entrances and give tempos. Possible depth and complexity are increased even more over a small ensemble. Tuttis become larger. You can fill larger venues with sound. There is less worry about players being exhausted during a long performance; there are still many opportunities for solos, improvisations, and places for individual players to shine. You can dedicate a single instrument to a character: a leading lady is routinely a flute, perhaps, or the villain always represented by the double bass. Choices do not need to be this predictable or cliché; you could do the opposite or something unexpected, keeping it consistent so the characterizations are understood. Beth Custer's score for *Chemi Bebia* (1929) is scored for seven instruments (Figure 3.2). Note the use of improvisation, with instructions simply entered as text in the bass clarinet and trumpet parts.

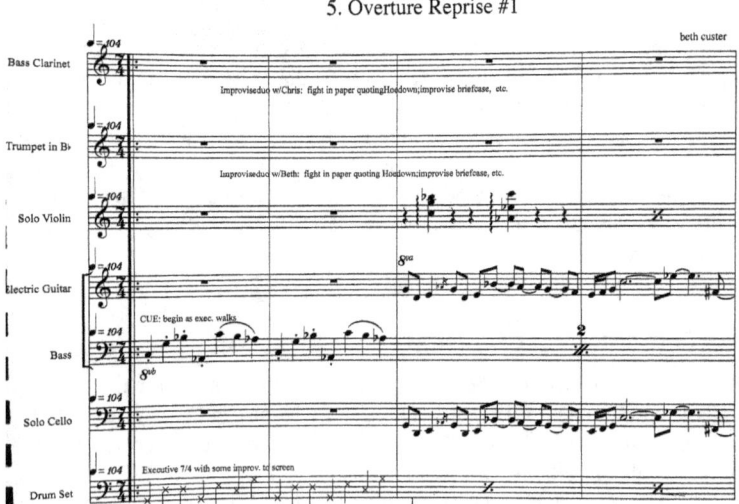

Figure 3.2 Live score for *Chemi Bebia (My Grandmother)* dir. by Kote Mikaberidze (1929), © Beth Custer 2005. Used by permission.

Orchestra

More than eight players situated before the screen becomes perceived as an orchestra by most audiences. Larger ensembles are best suited for larger venues that offer adequate space. You may need to visit venues beforehand to scope out where everyone will go. Large groups can feel unwieldy in rehearsal; large groups can respond more slowly to a conductor, unless players have significant orchestra experience.

Using an orchestra or large ensemble may *suggest* more conservative approaches, such as a fully notated score. This can reduce chaos, accidents, unpredictability, the number of rehearsals, and so on. If a score is fully notated, hired players can come in and play through it – whereas scores incorporating improvisation, mickey-mousing, and other ad lib techniques can require more rehearsals, coaching, even specialized players with expertise in free improvisation.

Orchestras and large ensembles can still employ approaches that are avant-garde, less reliant on traditional notation, or that eschew traditional notation altogether, such as *conduction*. Butch Morris (1947–2013) developed conduction as a technique to lead ensembles using a vocabulary of hand, body, and baton gestures. Others in New York's downtown scene, like John Zorn, developed their own similar techniques. When players understand the conductor's signals, they know when to play and can follow the gestures. Music can be made spontaneously or planned by the conductor in advance.

You might try having a large ensemble *without* a conductor; in this instance, you might divide the ensemble into sections, each with its own dramatic purpose, where section leaders synchronize tempos and entrances. The more you break down a large ensemble, you may be looking at more chaos or more rehearsal time. This could be a fun experiment for a large class, but if your goal is truly to give players more artistic freedom and independence, a smaller ensemble is likely the way to go.

With a large ensemble, we should think about the layout of players in rehearsal and performance, in particular *sight lines* and proximity to other performers. Does the player watch the screen or a conductor? Do they need to see both? Players do not need to be seated in a traditional orchestral layout; there are better ways of seating a large ensemble for silent film. Players who mickey-mouse important roles in scenes together might sit together, so they can dialogue and not step on each other's parts (notice the "improvised duo" specified in Figure 3.2). High instruments might be grouped together for better tuning and harmonization; it is difficult or impossible to retune during a long performance. A rhythm section might be grouped together, to help keep it tight; who this section includes depends on how you use different instruments.

If the conductor *faces the screen* and the ensemble faces the conductor – unless the group is angled sideways or players can turn around – players cannot see the screen and will therefore need to take all their cues from the conductor; this approach nearly requires a fully notated score and perhaps even a click track.

This setup can be reversed: players can face the screen, facilitating mickey-mousing and tight synchronization, with the conductor *facing the ensemble*. The conductor may use a tablet to see the screen behind them, or a video feed from the projection booth. Sightlines, visibility, and staging are further discussed in Chapter 4.

Depending upon the depth of the pit, height of the screen, and the pitch of auditorium seating, some instruments *might* block the screen and, if so, can be kept to one side; these instruments might include double bass and percussion. (Sometimes, self-conscious players can believe they are "in the way," when it is a really a non-issue from the point of view of the audience.) You may also need to be mindful of light splash on the screen from poorly positioned stand lights from raised instruments.

Dividing duties among players

Given an ensemble with multiple players, a composer might consider how to best deploy available forces. Some instruments may be suited for particular roles or characters, especially with mickey-mousing or important solos. If an instrumentalist can double, or an electronic keyboard has multiple patches, this widens the sound palette, but the composer must ascertain *when* to use *what sound*. A matrix of possibilities for instruments, characters, themes, and specialized duties (like conducting or controlling electronics) may result in a puzzle of how to best deploy forces at hand.

It may make sense to save particular sounds for special moments. *Sunrise: A Song of Two Humans* features a pivotal church wedding scene; while organ is a bread-and-butter silent movie sound, consider the added impact if it is used *only* for this scene.

Tuttis, especially at *fortissimo*, offer the loudest, largest moments or sonic blasts; these should be planned in advance; and other sections scaled around them. It's wise to let the score breathe, including opportunities for solos, duets, and trios, rather than having a constant barrage of sound.

Exercises or thought experiments

Choose a silent film.

1. Create a rough cue list for the film.
2. Where would you want *tuttis*?

3. Where could you keep the music smaller or sparser?
4. How would you prioritize certain sounds or character roles with a limited set of players?

Exploiting or avoiding clichés

As discussed in the section on solo piano, even one hundred years after the silent era, audiences still harbor expectations of "silent film music": a warbly theater organ, or an out of tune piano, mining stock gestures from Ernö Rapée. While I focus on *contemporary* scoring techniques, it's worth taking a moment to recall earlier approaches.

Rapée and others published compendiums of sheet music to generate ideas and examples for silent film accompaniment.[9] Sometimes, movie studios and music publishers would send out "cue sheets" for particular films, often two or three pages of lead sheet melodies and their suggested placements.[10] These form an actual historical basis for our audience expectations of "silent film music."

"Silent film music" clichés often comprise musical shorthand that pairs well with established cinematic tropes. In the video *Music for the Movies: The Hollywood Sound*, musicologist David Neumeyer demonstrates (on piano) the use of a tremolo diminished 7th chord to represent villainy.[11] This gesture is completely corny. Such clichés are not all bad, nor all good. Knowing and recognizing common cinematic tropes, you can plan in advance how to accompany them. There may be situations in which falling back on a facile cliché isn't so bad, and other cases where you may wish to *avoid* clichés.

The Golem highlights scenes of wizardry and magic, as well as religious piety and strictures. A wealth of clichés is available to be exploited; which should be used? Which should be avoided? Do you want to make the wizardry look otherworldly or silly? What supports the film best?

Metropolis shows fanciful, futuristic machinery, including the imposing Heart Machine; there are many models for mechanistic musical composition. How have others approached tropes of machinery?[12] Does this always need to be some kind of *ostinato*? Are there unique and creative approaches that you can employ to distinguish your own music?

One cliché I have found particularly useful is pizzicato bass for *sneaks*. Whenever a character is sneaking around, snooping, or searching, pizzicato just works. Your bassist can play almost anything slow pizz, and there you have your sneaks. Choosing interesting musical material can alleviate the corniness; what if these pizzes all belong to an atonal *pitch set*? Then again, you may hate this cliché and wish to avoid it altogether.

Timing: leading, coinciding, or following

How you time music to onscreen events is critical, as this directly impacts audience response. Timing is especially a concern in live performance; in practice, there will always be slight discrepancies in the execution of a live score. Awareness of how you'd like music to line up with onscreen action is essential; this timing should be carefully planned and rehearsed with allowances for variances in live performance. Timing issues are not unique to silent film, and remain a concern in contemporary cinema.

Music can *lead*, music can be *spot on* (like a *jump scare*), or music can *follow*. When something is *about to happen*, do you want music to *give it away*? Does music create suspense, does it *lead*, building audience expectation? Or does music wait, allowing the story to unfold and reveal itself, allowing onscreen action to surprise the audience? What signals does music send to the audience, or does it withhold them? (Some directors do not like music to give away what is going to happen, especially if they feel the picture cut already tells the story effectively.)

In *Dr. Jekyll and Mr. Hyde*, one might ponder, at what point during Dr. Jekyll's first transformation might music indicate something is awry (ca. 00:27:00)? What is the effect if (1) music *leads*, (2) music is *tightly timed*, or (3) music *lags*, letting the audience *see* John Barrymore's transformation unprompted, then coinciding with *audience response*? Overplaying or *anticipating* a dramatic point may ruin the moment for people who have never seen the film. There's no right or wrong answer, just various possibilities. How do different approaches to timing affect a scene?

We can look at timing on a broader scale, relating to musical development across an entire motion picture. This is especially germane in cases where there is strong character development or progressive revelations. In *Nosferatu*, how might you play Count Orlock's first entrance, at dusk, at his castle (ca. 00:22:40)? Do we need to immediately know his intentions? This question applies not to immediate situational timing (like the Dr. Jekyll example), but rather to timing Orlock's development *over the course of the whole film*. When Orlock first appears, he has already been established by reputation (the carriage driver won't approach his castle; villagers shudder at his name). But, at this point, Orlock seems noble, cold, and aloof, if tall and intimidating. How might music track his development over the course of the film? What do we want to impart (or hold back) to the audience at Orlock's first entrance? How would we play subsequent scenes with Orlock? How would we play him by the end of the film?

Exercises or thought experiments

Find a scene with a dramatic *reveal* or some kind of sudden action.

1. Score the scene, having music lead or "tip off" the audience.
2. Score the scene, having music tightly timed, like a *jump scare*.
3. Score the scene, having the music lag, aiming to allow the music to react in tandem with an audience's reaction.
4. Compare these approaches, and how well they work for your particular chosen scene. Would the results be different for a different scene? Why?

Work on timing in performance. Take a look at that Dr. Jekyll transformation scene, or pick another scene that has some kind of *reveal* in it. Compose a brief piece of music for it, and then see how well you can time it in live performance.

1. Find places where you can cushion the score to help with synchronization.
2. Find an area where music can start anywhere and still work.
3. Find an area where music can finish anywhere and still work.

If you have a musical or dramatic climax within the start and finish, how tightly can you place it?

Choose a silent feature with a central character who develops over the course of the film. Can you write a theme that would grow or develop over the course of the film to match that? Would it begin with a *fragment*? How would it grow or change?

Environmental effects

While composers enjoy playing emotion and concocting powerful, memorable movie themes, a score is denser and richer when composers exploit *other* opportunities as well. Some players can handle *environmental effects* even while others simultaneously play themes or emotions. These effects give the score subtlety and dimensionality.

Sounds of the sea, air, wind, heat, cold, running water, splashes, steam, and so on can be handled musically. Woodwinds offer effects like colored noise and third octave overtones. Buzzing reeds and mouthpieces can be insects and animal creatures. Strings have creak tone (sub-harmonics), harmonics, *col legno, jeté, sul ponticello* and other effects that make sounds ranging from a whisper to a convincing door knock. These effects are discussed in detail in orchestration books like Adler's *The Study of Orchestration*, Blatter's *Instrumentation and Orchestration*, Solomon's *How to Write for Percussion*, and others.

Sunrise: A Song of Two Humans, with obvious openings for emotional scoring, offers other opportunities for musical interpretation: the storm, the streetcar, the runaway pig, shouting crowds, honking horns, a bicycle bell in city traffic. These are all story elements. If these important bits of story are brought forward musically, the film becomes much more *alive*.

Nosferatu, likewise, has important environmental elements: buzzing mosquitos, the steep Carpathian Mountains, the windy beach, rolling ocean waves, the derelict house, the cold castle. Music can emphasize these qualities, even as a theme or melody is played by other instruments simultaneously.

Exercises or thought experiments

Choose a feature-length silent film.

1. Take note of where you could use environmental effects.
2. What kinds of instruments or extended techniques could best create those effects?
3. Would those effects work well as a bed for other more prominent music on top? How might they combine with thematic, melodic material played simultaneously?

Emotional readings

Focusing on environmental effects helps a composer avoid overplaying emotion. Silent films imply strong emotions to contemporary audiences, but this does not always need amplification. Avoid milking every moment. By exercising restraint, a contemporary score can make a silent film more genuine, resonant, and less corny.

As discussed in Chapter 1, silent film acting tends to telegraph emotion through established gestures that are clear – if you understand the gestures. If gestures are subtle or likely to be misunderstood, they may benefit from emotional music. If the gestures are unambiguous, pedaling emotional music too hard may just pile it on unnecessarily.

In *Dr. Jekyll and Mr. Hyde*, Millie, Utterson, Lanyon, and their associates try to get a read on what's going on with Dr. Jekyll. Millie vacillates between concern, disappointment, thoughtfulness: she has to negotiate two marriage proposals, balancing her father's wishes, her own heart, and what seems sensible. As a result, there are several scenes that traffic in the ambiguities and complexities of the moment (ca. 00:07:00; ca. 00:12:50; ca. 00:23:40; 00:38:00). If you write powerful emotional music for such delicate scenes, you may do the film a disservice by forcing a particular interpretation.

A composer should study a film to gauge emotional readings, whether they need help, and whether they are monochromatic or complex. A character may appear *sad*, but they may also be expressing concern or contemplation. Imagining a character's interior monologue, as discussed in Chapter 1, helps a composer consider more complex ways of playing a scene, rather than simply scoring abject sadness. Music can reflect the emotional depth *and* complexity of a film.

Exercises or thought experiments

Find a dialogue scene in a silent film, especially one where the situation or gestures are a bit subtle or ambiguous.

1. As an exercise, try scoring the scene with a variety of heavy-handed emotional approaches. If you make the music deliberately sad, angry, happy, or fearful, does it clash with the scene? Does it bring out certain moments?
2. Try scoring the scene with music that *shifts* emotional register during the scene. What points call for a change?
3. Try scoring the scene with a bed of music throughout that shows great restraint, that may even be *bland*.

Which approach works best? Can you combine the approaches? Did any of the approaches change the perceptible *meaning* of the scene or the implications of the dialogue?

Hallucinations and dream sequences

Hallucinations, dream sequences, fantasy sequences, flashbacks, and flash forwards all offer intriguing musical opportunities; these are places where music can differ from the rest of the score, in order to distinguish these sections from normality.

In *Dr. Jekyll and Mr. Hyde*, Dr. Jekyll's visit to the opium den provides an opportunity to accentuate the drug haze (ca. 00:45:20). *The Phantom Carriage* has multiple scenes in the otherworld, or underwater (ca. 00:22:50), that can be differentiated from normal waking life. *Daisy Doodad's Dial* shows a dream sequence where Daisy is haunted by a parade of her own grimacing visage (ca. 00:07:50). These scenes provide opportunities where music can take the audience into a markedly different space.

There are many musical techniques to choose from, or to combine, that create transformational spaces for the audience. You might consider unusual modes or scales (like Locrian, whole tone, or octatonic). You can use this as an opportunity to change instrumentation, especially if you have multi-instrumentalists. Consider using specialized instruments just for these scenes; you can have players switch to recorders, mouthpieces, kazoos, ocarinas, percussion, homemade instruments, or any unusual instruments they may have access to. You can also use regular instruments in unusual ways: playing low on soprano instruments (consider the fogginess of low trumpet), or high on low instruments (the audible strain of a cello or bass bowed very high). You can employ extended techniques, making unusual sounds. You can change the *density* of the arrangement; perhaps it becomes exaggeratedly thick, or very sparse. Exercise your freedom and creativity, while avoiding clichés if you can. Making sounds the audience cannot readily identify can make a score pop and add to onscreen mysteries.

Comedy

Like emotional moments discussed above, comedy risks being musically overplayed. When watching a film, consider: what are the jokes? What is *supposed* to be funny? Ideally, the audience should laugh at *intended jokes*, rather than laughing *at the film itself*. You want to bring the audience *into* the world of the film, not take them out of it. (You may recall how *film funning*, discussed in Chapter 2, can take an audience out of the film, an approach this book actively discourages.)

When you have identified light or comedic moments, consider how much help they need. Will they work better *without* exaggerating goofiness or mining clichés? (Note this question persists today in scoring comedy!)

Another pitfall is to *ignore* comedy altogether, to treat an entire silent film as a museum piece with no sense of humor. Weighty, canonical films *do* have moments that serve as comedic reprieves. *Sunrise: A Song of Two Humans* has a number of funny vignettes: the escaped pig, the drunk waiter, the photo shop escapade. You can hit these comedic moments and still treat the film with respect. If you ignore comedic moments, a film can feel too ponderous or unintentionally pretentious.

Moments with comedic *potential* add complexity to a film. In a tense café scene in *Sunrise*, the Man feebly attempts to patch things up, bringing his distraught Wife a plate of cakes (ca. 00:37:10). But the plate of cakes is *far too big*; it doesn't make sense from a practical standpoint. The Man is a bit of a hayseed, not the sharpest tack in the box, and the number of cakes seems like overcompensation. There is a desperate magnanimity to the gesture, as if the cakes were atonement for attempted murder. But any laughs are quickly deflated as the Wife starts to cry in the café, and they have to leave.

The character of Knock in *Nosferatu* provides some *comic relief*. He overacts his joy at sending Hutter on a fool's errand (ca. 00:08:00), and ends up eating flies in jail (ca. 00:45:50). At times sadistic, avaricious, or having lost his mind (bringing up ethical issues of how to play mental illness), Knock provides moments that can be played for comedy – or not. How you navigate Knock is an example of how scoring comedy deserves careful consideration.

Chases

A basic cinematic *trope*, the chase is typically handled musically with some form of *scherzo*. Chases are usually easy to spot and may coincide with an accelerated visual pace or picture cuts. Chases may provide opportunities for increased improvisation, variation of established themes, *conduction*, or any combination of these.

Consider the purposes of the chase: is it a gratuitous action sequence? Does it tell us something about the characters? In *Sunrise*, The Wife runs from The Man, letting us know that she has figured out that he is dangerous (ca. 00:32:00). The Man gives chase, but we have yet to ascertain fully his intentions or what is unfolding. Later in the film, the Man chases the runaway pig, but this is played for comedy and ersatz country heroism.

You don't *need* to score a chase with a scherzo; The Wife's flight from The Man could be played with some form of sadness; it could be a twisted variation of a theme for The Man; it could be music that reflects the woodsy environment and remains detached from the chase itself. In all cases, you might consider the purpose of the chase within the film, and how your music can reinforce that purpose.

Exercises or thought experiments

Find a chase sequence in a silent film.

1. Describe what is going on dramatically, the reason for the chase sequence in the film.
2. Score the chase as an action sequence using a scherzo.
3. Make the tempo follow the speed of the chase.
4. Score the chase for multiple instruments, using improvisatory instructions. (Consult the section on *structured improvisation* in Chapter 4 if needed.)
5. Score the chase using music or instructions that *avoid* a scherzo feel. What is the effect? What does it focus attention on by doing it this way?

The end

A film's ending provides opportunities to restate important themes or provide a satisfying musical *climax* or *resolution*. Sound films with spoken dialogue may not always offer the chance to conclude with a full recapitulation or reiteration of an important musical theme. In silent film, you have more leeway to do that.

Music in a final scene may encourage the audience to read a film in a particular way, or even to reconsider the whole film. The ending of *Nosferatu* implies this is really *Ellen's* story, even if more *screen time* was devoted to Hutter's misadventures. The ending of *Dr. Jekyll and Mr. Hyde* centers Dr. Jekyll, even if Hyde was the more interesting character. The ending of *Sunrise* features the titular sunrise, lending important symbolism to the rebirth of the troubled marriage.

Silent films often end abruptly; a card announces "Fin" or "The End" without ensuing end credits, so the musical finish should be carefully timed. The ending may be a moment to *avoid* improvisation and to keep your players together, powerful, with parts simple, *allargando*, coming to rest in a big finish. This may be overly conventional, and you are welcome to try other approaches, but it does well to reinforce the ending of a film.

Exercises or thought experiments

Choose a silent film ending.

1. Calculate timings for the ending. How long is the final scene? How long is the concluding shot or moment? How long does it hold until the "The End" card appears?
2. Plan music for the ending moment; try working this out *in reverse*. At what point do you want the music to end? At what point would you need the final chord or fermata to begin? What screen action would indicate a good sync point for a final phrase? What point would be a safe place for a concluding theme to start?
3. Try playing along and see how comfortable these timings work out. Is it easy or tricky? If it's too tricky to get right every time, what would make it easier?

Notes

1 Altman, Rick. (2004). *Silent Film Sound*. (New York: Columbia University Press). pp. 85–7.
2 London, Kurt. Translated by Eric S. Bensinger. (1936). *Film Music: A Summary of the Characteristic Features of Its History, Aesthetics, Technique; and Possible Developments*. (London: Faber & Faber Ltd.). p. 40.

Consider your score   83

3   Rapée, Ernö. (1924). *Motion Picture Moods for Pianists and Organists.* (New York: G. Schirmer, Inc.).
4   See https://www.youtube.com/watch?v=WcDDmwVdSlw
5   Altman, Rick. (2004). *Silent Film Sound.* (New York: Columbia University Press). pp. 330–7.
6   See https://www.edisonstudio.it/en/home-en/
7   A good resource for these techniques is Roads, Curtis. (2023). *The Computer Music Tutorial*, Second Edition. (Cambridge, MA: The MIT Press).
8   See https://www.lookmumnocomputer.com
9   See Rapée, Ernö. (1924). *Motion Picture Moods For Pianists and Organists.* (New York: G. Schirmer, Inc.). See also Erdmann, Hans, Becce, Giuseppe, and Brav, Ludwig. (1927). *Allgemeines Handbuch der Film-Musik.* (Berlin-Lichterfelde, Leipzig: Schlesinger). (2020 reprint: Berlin: Ries & Erler).
10 Many of these are preserved at the *Silent Film Sound & Music Archive* website under the Cue Sheets category at www.sfsma.org
11 *Music for the Movies: The Hollywood Sound.* (1995). Video. Director Joshua Waletzky. (West Branch, NJ: Kultur Video).
12 Iconic examples include Raymond Scott's "Powerhouse" often heard in Warner Brothers cartoons.

Bibliography

Dubowsky, Jack C. (2011). "The Evolving "Temp Score" in Animation." *Music, Sound, and the Moving Image*, Vol. 5, No. 1. Spring (Liverpool: Liverpool University Press).

Erdmann, Hans, Becce, Giuseppe, and Brav, Ludwig. (1927). *Allgemeines Handbuch der Film-Musik* (Berlin-Lichterfelde, Leipzig: Schlesinger) (2020 reprint: Berlin: Ries & Erler).

Music for the Movies: The Hollywood Sound. (1995). Video. Director Joshua Waletzky (West Long Branch NJ: Kultur Video).

Rapée, Ernö. (1924). *Motion Picture Moods for Pianists and Organists* (New York: G. Schirmer, Inc.).

Saunders, Alfred H., Editor. (1911, July 22). "Our Music Page." *The Moving Picture News*, Vol. IV, No. 29 (New York: The Cinematograph Publishing Company), p. 9.

Shockley, Alan (2018). *The Contemporary Piano: A Performer and Composer's Guide to Techniques and Resources* (Lanham, MD: Rowman & Littlefield.).

4 Communicate your score

This chapter looks at ways to document and communicate your score to your players, and ultimately, the audience. We look at musical approaches to scoring, including stylistic options, methods of notation, and conducting concerns.

Compositional style, tonal language, musical approaches

After we have studied and spotted a film as described in Chapter 2, and we have planned and sketched themes as described in Chapter 3, we may further reflect upon musical approaches we might take. Electroclash? Free jazz? Hip hop? No wave? Should the film have a certain sound or musical approach?

Performing a live score to silent film creates opportunities to explore creative possibilities and to *defy common presumptions* of what "film music" should sound like: that it requires an orchestra, a certain harmonic language, or a certain style. As of this writing, the "epic" style is overused – sample sets and music libraries even come *titled* "epic," implying that this is a sound that one can simply *buy*. In other periods, other styles were overused; see midcentury West Coast Jazz.[1]

I encourage you to discover and use your *own compositional voice* to create a unique sound and approach, rather than imitate what everyone else is doing. Secondly, as crazy, outré, strange, or avant-garde as your music might be, I hope it will *respect the director's intentions* and vision, and *support the film* in telling the story the director had in mind.

Avant-garde

Composing for silent film affords us artistic possibilities to shatter audience preconceptions and clichéd expectations. Writing in 1941, expatriate German-Austrian composer and intellectual Hanns Eisler asked rhetorically,

> [I]s it really necessary to continue the current Hollywood practice of rehashing 'original' scores with crumbs picked from the tables of Tchaikowsky [sic], Debussy, Ravel, Richard Strauss and Stravinsky? Is new musical material possible? May it not even be more useful and effective?[2]

Eisler, seeing "new musical material" as "more useful and effective" for film than "rehashing" known classics, composed music for several documentaries using a serial 12-tone style he learned studying with Arnold Schoenberg.

Others would push the envelope as well. Helen van Dongen created a full reel of musique concrète for *Louisiana Story* (1948), a sound collage of recordings made at an oil derrick; today this might be called noise music or industrial music, two genres underused in film music.[3] Bebe and Louis Barron, Gil Mellé, and Wendy Carlos composed atonal electronic music for film. Directors Stanley Kubrick and William Friedkin placed existing avant-garde classical music by composers György Ligeti and Krzysztof Penderecki in their films.

As early as 1941, Eisler noticed that audiences accepted and enjoyed atonal and avant-garde music in film.

> Apparently advanced musical material, which average concertgoers may find indigestible and non-relevant, when applied to films loses something of this forbidding quality. Even the unaccustomed ear finds complex musical devices more understandable and effective when accompanied by visual images.[4]

This phenomenon is logical: if music works to *support* the picture, if music and moving image *join together* effectively, the net effect overrides personal tastes and biases. Powerful cinema achieves a sort of idealized Wagnerian *Gesamtkunstwerk* through which audiences no longer concern themselves with details of musical genre, but absorb the *entire effect*.

Composing and performing music for silent film affords you freedoms and opportunities to be radically interesting in any number of ways. You are free from director, studio, or network notes. You don't need to avoid clashing with a dialogue track. You can make art. You can make mistakes. You can try things that push boundaries, and may succeed better than "crumbs picked from the tables" of established mainstream composers.

Exercises or thought experiments

Choose a three- to five-minute excerpt of a silent film.

1. Compose music in an electronic, atonal, serial, or otherwise avant-garde style.

Pastiche

It's possible to use a mix of styles throughout a film. Mixing contrasting musical styles is called *pastiche*, a term often applied to the work of John Corigliano, who composed concert works, the opera *The Ghosts of Versailles*, and scores for *The Red Violin* and *Altered States*.

Use of pastiche in film benefits from planned, *conceptual consistency*: rather than changing musical style at random, pastiche is best used to *emphasize cinematic aspects*. One might carefully switch styles based on locations, characters, or points in time.

In *Sunrise*, a thematic bifurcation separates city and countryside. The city is sophisticated, loud, noisy, and filled with temptation. The countryside is simple and homey. City folk vacation in the country; country folk long to see the city. *Sunrise* explores this duality as a major plot device. Could the city be loud, exciting bebop jazz, while the countryside is pastoral woodwind chorales?

Metropolis features an aboveground city and belowground city. Could the aboveground city be represented by a light, airy style, like bubblegum pop, and the belowground city by a heavier, darker style, like death metal?

Characters may be delineated by contrasting musical styles. Dr. Jekyll and Mr. Hyde are one man who undergoes a recurring transformation. Could you give them the same musical theme but radically change its style for each incarnation?

Movies that shift through time, like *Dr. Jekyll and Mr. Hyde* and *The Phantom Carriage*, could use different styles to reflect different time periods.

You may come up with other ideas for how to plan consistent use of pastiche. Contrasting musical styles can be tied to various elements of a film; hypothetically, you could employ any number of styles and connect them to things like certain special effects, particular cards, or distinctive close-ups.

Exercises or thought experiments

Choose a silent film.

1. Find ways to plan the use of pastiche. What would be effective aspects for differing, contrasting styles to latch on to? What would those styles be, and why?

Responsiveness and mickey-mousing

The term *mickey-mousing* derives from the Walt Disney Company's tight musical timing and innovative use of synchronized *bar charts* to guide composers in scoring animated cartoons.[5] Bar charts indicated moments of action, mapped out over bars and beats. This allowed composers to precisely hit their marks.[6]

Mickey-mousing came to mean a style of *carefully following or mimicking character actions or gestures*; this can be seen in films of all time periods: if a stack of cards topples over, the music falls with it. Such mickey-mousing is one end of a spectrum of how *responsive* a film score is, but it is an effective technique in scoring silent film.[7]

It is worthwhile to consider in advance how responsive a score might be, how much mickey-mousing might be incorporated, or, considering the other end of the responsiveness spectrum, how much is *mood music* – an unresponsive bed of music that serves to set the tone for a scene or a sequence.[8] It is possible to operate anywhere on this spectrum, and even to have *both*: some players might create an ambience or mood, while another player follows and imitates a character closely. This way, you can have overlapping layers of theme and mickey-mousing, creating a richer, more complex score.

While imitative musical gestures can be written out in precise musical notation, these gestures can be accomplished effectively through structured improvisation, discussed below.

You can get good results when players mickey-mouse in tandem. In *The Mark of Zorro*, Douglas Fairbanks as Don Diego Vega performs little goofy tricks with his hat and handkerchiefs – childlike, joke shop kind of immature gags. As his hat flies around and zips back, this could be doubled with slide guitar *and* slide whistle. Why not use both? It makes the sound more comical and unique.

In many films, you have shots of people crying or laughing. Using instruments to their idiomatic advantage, you could have one instrument, like a flute, handle character movement and dialogue, while a clarinet performs crying, sobbing, or laughing, for which it is particularly well suited. In this case, two instruments work together to create an overall character effect.

Exercises or thought experiments

Find a part of a silent film that has people or objects moving, falling, or exhibiting some kind of kinetic action.

1. Compose, perform, or improvise some music that tracks that action closely.

Find a silent film dialogue scene where a character or characters emote clearly with clear expressions.

1. Compose, perform, or improvise some music that tracks their dialogue.
2. Try having this music continue over cards that show what is being said.
3. Try mickey-mousing a scene with another player, each taking their own role. Try to leave space for each other. Emphasize which player represents which character. Try not to play over each other, unless that is called for by the scene.

Improvisation

Improvisation has a long history in silent film, being part and parcel of its earliest accompaniment. (Once movie palaces were built, and studios could provide sheet music for house orchestras, notated scores became fashionable.) Film music historian Kurt London, writing in 1933, recalled early silent film accompanists:

> [T]he better musicians frequently improvised. They abandoned themselves to their moods, as prompted by the pictures, and expressed them in a medley of their own and other people's music, free from any convention of style. They thereby had recourse instinctively to an ideal form of silent-film music: *improvisation*. But this form was destined to remain a solecism, and it naturally fell into disuse as the average cinema grew larger.[9]

It is interesting to ponder why recorded scores of the *sound period* continued to rely on fully notated music. There are exceptions – sound films with improvised music or scores incorporating improvisation include Quincy Jones' 1964 score for *The Pawnbroker* – but these are less common, even though improvisations could be recorded and edited on fixed media, providing a final result that is still studio-controlled.

Much silent period improvisation involved the *choice* of material to play – pulling from popular songs, themes from mood compendiums like Erdmann[10] or Rapée[11] – and then working out transitions, endings, interludes, and generally *conforming* chosen selections to the picture. There are other forms of improvisation as well. We will look in particular at structured improvisation, motivic improvisation, idiomatic improvisation, as well as soloing. As we make distinctions between forms of improvisation, remember they are not mutually exclusive: structured improvisation can incorporate existing motives, and so forth.

Structured improvisation

Mickey-mousing, ambiences, and sound effects do not need to be entirely notated; in many cases, it's best if they are *not* notated at all.

A percussionist duplicating hits in a swordfight can *perform those better ad lib* than you can notate them. Wind players can create environmental wind effects freely. A player imitating physical movement or language – pleading, crying, laughing, arguing, shouting – can improvise those gestures without complicated notation.

These improvisations are *structured improvisation*, where the film itself provides the structure. The idea is to support and synchronize to the *film – not* to follow a chord chart (as one might improvise a "solo" in jazz or pop music). In fact, much *structured improvisation* for silent film works better when it is *atonal*, or ventures outside key areas other musicians might play simultaneously (a notated character theme, for instance). This atonality or different pitch set distinguishes mickey-mousing from its musical surroundings, so it doesn't disappear in the mix, or sound like another part of a musical fabric. You want it to stand out, so the audience takes notice. Structured improvisation follows its own visual and narrative cues; performing structured improvisation is its own skillset, and can be refined in rehearsal so it works with the film.

Timing of improvisation is crucial, and relies on players' willingness to carefully study the film. Often these gestures need to be *dead on* to work. Matching screen action is essential; a player should be momentarily free from the written score to *follow the screen* independent of whatever the rest of the band is playing. Therefore, the use of improvisation leads us to consider notation techniques, which are discussed later in this chapter.

Exercises or thought experiments

Find a scene or sequence in a silent film. Try using these onscreen vectors to structure improvisation. Imagine other possibilities.

1. Dialogue. How can dialogue provide a structure for improvisation? Include both onscreen speaking as well as intertitle cards that show what's being said. Try this with multiple players and characters. Try to leave space for each other.
2. Weather. Consider the storm scene in *Sunrise* (ca. 01:14:30). It starts with a light rain in The City, and gets worse and worse. How can players track this, with the weather structuring their improvisation? Could multiple players take different aspects?
3. Lightness and darkness. Can the lighting of a scene – from bright and sunny to dark and creepy – structure some elements of improvisation? How would it affect playing?
4. Action and impacts. In a fight or action scene, can blows, speed, confusion, and so on structure what is played?
5. Tension. If a situation becomes tense, can a player improvise that tension?
6. Can you have multiple players tracking each of these, as applicable, all at once? What would that sound like?

Motivic improvisation

In composing for silent film, you may come up with strong themes you really like. The idea behind *motivic improvisation* – distinct from soloing or *comping* over chord changes – is that players freely manipulate *thematic and motivic melodic material* as the basis for improvisation, *without* necessarily adhering to any chord chart or progression. This makes the manipulation more free, creative, and developmental, while still pointing to existing composed themes.

Themes can be broken down into *fragments*; these might be a phrase, a bar, or two bars of a longer melody. Distinctive fragments provide good material for manipulation. This way, a musician can freely improvise around a musical idea without wearing out a theme's welcome. The full realization of the theme can be held in abeyance until an important moment in the film.

Fragments, motives, and themes can be manipulated through exploring *melodic contour*, rhythmic figuration, rhythmic augmentation and diminution, melodic inversion, reversal, reharmonization, and so on. These techniques are discussed in many composition texts; my point here is that such manipulation can be done on the fly, freely, in improvisation. Furthermore, these thematic fragments can be introduced within the course of *other* improvisational techniques.

Structural improvisation can incorporate both gestural improvisation and melodic improvisation. Imagine a player mickey-mousing Florence Turner's outlandish facial gestures in *Daisy Doodad's Dial* (1914) using *fragments of a theme*, rather than just squawks and slides. You can imagine a chase scene where a short fragment of a character's theme is *sped up* and repeated to match the pace of the action.

This book encourages approaches that give individual players freedom to interpret silent film and express their ideas musically. Still, and especially in a group ensemble, this improvisation often needs to be coached.

Exercises or thought experiments

Find or choose a musical theme. It can be something you have written, a well-known movie theme, a classical tune, or a familiar song melody. The theme should ideally be several phrases long, something called a *period* in classical western music theory. Something 8 to 16 bars long is about the right length.

1. Identify several *fragments* within the theme. The idea is to identify little musical snippets that are, independently, musical building blocks of the overall tune.
2. Vary, develop, or otherwise manipulate a fragment. Consider how you might play with rhythm, melodic contour, direction or inversion, modality, texture, and so on.
3. Extend the fragment through repetition as well as variation.

4. Construct new material generated exclusively from that fragment.
5. Try another fragment from the theme. See which fragments lend themselves to development. What works best? What kind of manipulation makes them interesting but still recognizable? What kind of manipulation makes them unrecognizable?
6. Try improvising on or varying a longer segment of the theme, maybe a whole phrase, four to eight bars.

Coaching improvisation

If you lead your own ensemble, you may need to coach improvisation in order to get the right approach, result, and characterizations. How you coach improvisation depends on the kind of player you are coaching. As an overbroad generalization and oversimplification, I present three categories of improvisers, for the purpose of discussing coaching silent film improvisation. These are the *classical musician* who is primarily trained to read, the musician from a *jazz or pop background* who is primarily trained to improvise over a chord chart, and the *free improviser* who may come already skilled in creative approaches but needs work in ensemble playing or following a film.

Classical musicians – those from western traditions accustomed to reading fully notated parts – may need to be drawn out from shyness or reserve. They may benefit from simple exercises or games, like playing *high* or playing *low*, or playing *loud* or playing *soft*, depending on how *bright the screen glows*, or how *high you raise your hand*. Anything to take their minds off what they are playing (as far as pitch, key, melody) and allowing them to make sound and noise. Experimental films, like the *Five Film Exercises* by John and James Whitney, are great for this: players can be challenged to tempo-match the speed of the visuals, or play anything but *only* when they see a *certain color*.

Players from jazz, funk, rock, and popular music foundations provide a particular challenge, as they tend to view improvisation as "soloing" over chord changes in a chart. This approach has musical validity and opportunities for showcasing virtuosity, but the problem for silent film is that it tends to center the player rather than support the film. Or, these solos disappear into the musical bed without clearly connecting to onscreen action. The challenge is to coach these players to *ignore* tonality, to ignore what other people may be playing, and to venture outside key areas, outside established tempos, and to follow onscreen action tightly in a gestural way. You can use the same exercises described above. You can have pop-rock-jazz players make *sounds* following onscreen action *without anyone else playing*, so there is no chart, no musical background, encouraging them to use improvisation as a means to escape tonality. Following that, move them towards performing *atonal* improvisations that mimic onscreen action, while trampling over *tonal* material (a character theme or mood music) that *others* might be playing.

You want to take players steeped in popular tonal genres out of what guitarist and author Derek Bailey calls "idiomatic improvisation:" regurgitating common tropes whose form and material derive from established genre expectations and clichéd idiosyncrasies of an instrument.[12] Idiomatic improvisation can feel like random noodling when set to silent film: random not because it's failing to follow a chart (which it may follow perfectly well), but because it is *not following onscreen action*. There's often a place for idiomatic improvisation, but it tends to fall flat for mickey-mousing characters or action.

Experienced improvisers and established musicians on the free improv or creative music scenes may still need to learn to perform appropriate characterizations and to listen to and make space for other players. They may still be learning to take direction and to better understand the *film*, rather than just seeing live score as an unbridled opportunity for self-expression. Experienced improvisers can end up being your strongest players, but you may need to frame coaching in terms of the direction you want in characterization, emphasis, and tone, as well as what onscreen action deserves attention, where subtlety is called for, and structuring dynamics.

Notation techniques

The type of notation you use impacts how much rehearsal time you need, how much time players need to study their parts, how *identical* or *unique* live performances are, and how easily they are executed. This section examines various notation types and how they affect score preparation, rehearsal time, and live performance.

Fully notated score with extracted parts

The most formalized western tradition of communicating a live score is a *fully notated score* with extracted parts for each musician, telling them exactly what to play. This requires some time composing, arranging, and copying; disciplined rehearsal; and a conductor who makes sure the score stays synchronized. This system should lead to highly reproducible performances, but if there's no room for players' creativity or input, you may have to outright hire them.

There *are* ways of making a fully notated score somewhat adaptable. In Richard Marriott and Gino Robair's score for *Nosferatu* (Figure 4.1), you can see that two vamps are used (as well as a repeat; if the repeat is not needed, you can just take it out). The vamps will repeat until the conductor gives the signal to continue. This helps fill time and account for variations in tempo.

Communicate your score 93

Figure 4.1 *Nosferatu* full score © 1989 by Richard Marriott and Gino Robair. Note the use of Repeat 1, Vamp A, and Vamp B. Vamps help a conductor fit a live score precisely to the picture, even with an orchestra.

Exercises or thought experiments

Find a silent film scene. Notice structural points you would like music to accent.

1. Write some *notated* music for the scene (this can be for just one instrument). Use *vamps* to fill time between the structural events. Try using vamps of different lengths: one bar, two bars, up to four bars. What works best?
2. How can you make a vamp less obvious? Can you incorporate first and second endings, or allow an instrument to solo ad lib over the vamp?

Lead sheet

Lead sheets communicate a lot of information in a small space. They can be read by many players, including those in a traditional jazz or pop "rhythm section," like guitar, bass, banjo, and piano. In Figure 4.2, you can imagine a melodic instrument might take the melody; a guitar or keyboard might *comp* an accompaniment implied by the chord chart, paying attention to extended harmonies, like ninths; and a bass or low instrument might anchor the root notes. A flute or oboe might play the tune an octave up. The lead sheet can be seen as a guide to a fuller arrangement players realize appropriately.

If your group is a little bigger, you might include an extra voice or part. This is not strictly necessary; a very good player may be able to comp an implied interior line by ear, or through their knowledge of counterpoint and music theory. If that part isn't quite what you had in mind, a second voice fits nicely on the staff, as shown in Figure 4.3. It also can provide an alternative melody, for a variation.

Figure 4.4 shows the same lead sheet, transposed for B♭ instruments. Some players of B♭ instruments (like clarinet or trumpet) may be able to read

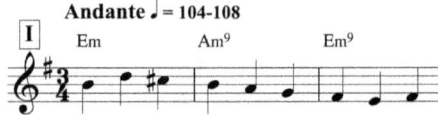

Figure 4.2 Lead sheet. Excerpt from "Millie" from *Dr. Jekyll and Mr. Hyde* by Jack Curtis Dubowsky © 2018 De Stijl Music.

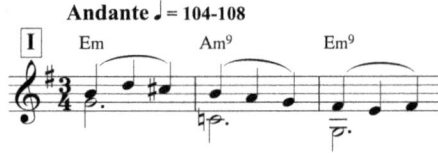

Figure 4.3 Lead sheet with second voice. Excerpt from "Millie" from *Dr. Jekyll and Mr. Hyde* by Jack Curtis Dubowsky © 2018 De Stijl Music.

Figure 4.4 Lead sheet with second voice transposed for B♭ instruments. Excerpt from "Millie" from *Dr. Jekyll and Mr. Hyde* by Jack Curtis Dubowsky © 2018 De Stijl Music.

a simple score in concert key, transposing their part at sight, but this should never be presumed.

Short score

With a small ensemble, musicians can play directly from an annotated *short score*: low voices take bass clef; high voices take high parts; middle voices navigate interior lines. One benefit is that players' parts, if complex, do not need courtesy cue notes; players can see on the page what others are playing.

A simple short score is shown in Figure 4.5. There is deliberately no chord chart in this example, but it clearly shows the arrangement in three to four voices. The second ending of [B] is shown in a cue-sized note, with a clarifying "f 2nd x" comment; this economizes the score. The ossia measures, a cue-sized third staff floating above [A], show how the score should be realized in four-part harmony, giving it an alternate realization.

Figure 4.6 shows a short score in two staves, condensing what could be up to four independent parts. You'll notice that stem direction helps differentiate the three parts in the treble clef.

Figure 4.5 Short score. "Love Theme" from *The Mark of Zorro* by Jack Curtis Dubowsky © 2017 De Stijl Music.

Figure 4.6 A short score in two staves. Excerpt from *Nosferatu* by Jack Curtis Dubowsky © 2018 De Stijl Music.

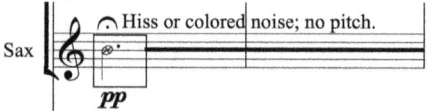

Figure 4.7 Box notation. Excerpt from *Mist* by Jack Curtis Dubowsky © 2013 De Stijl Music.

A drawback to short score is that some players may be distracted by having to *find their part* among others'. They would rather just see their own part. Short score works best with a small ensemble, or with a score that incorporates abbreviations or improvisation. One type of abbreviation is *box notation*.

Box notation

Box notation is a contemporary practice seen in the scores of John Corigliano and others (see Figure 4.7). Any desired effect or gesture that continues over time can be put in a box, and a line or arrow indicates its duration. An environmental effect, a section of mickey-mousing, frightened string tremolos, or an agitated scherzo figure, can all be put inside boxes, saving space on the page and simplifying the score.

Notice that *rests are removed*; ideally, rests should *not* appear when a player is playing, even if there is no standard notation for that bit. To avoid confusion, rests should always indicate a player is resting.

Text instructions

Instead of carefully notating a frightened string tremolo and putting it in a box, one can just write "frightened trems" and give *that* to string players. They will know what to do. Likewise, an environmental effect or mickey-mousing section can be handled this way. You can simply put a character's name in a musician's part – "Ellen" – and they will use that as a cue to "play" or mickey-mouse that character. This may require direction or coaching by the composer to indicate *how* that character should be played: is Ellen frightened or suspicious? Do you like the player's interpretation, or does it need to be toned down or adjusted?

Referring back to Chapter 3, Figure 2, you can see how composer Beth Custer simply dropped text instructions into the bass clarinet and trumpet parts: "Improvise duo w/Chris: fight in paper quoting Hoedown; improvise briefcase, etc." We would have to see the film for the instructions to make complete sense, but in just a few words Custer has stated clearly what she wants, without having to bother with detailed notation. (Note that this score would be clearer with the rests removed in those parts.)

Word score

Players that know a film well, have a strong musical memory, and can think about music verbally can write out a *word score* that documents what they want. Below, Figure 4.8, is a page from Terry Donahue's part to the Alloy Orchestra's score for *Metropolis*. Donahue explains this is "Just my percussion/accordion parts. You might be able to tell that for me the score is largely memorized with little reminders."[13]

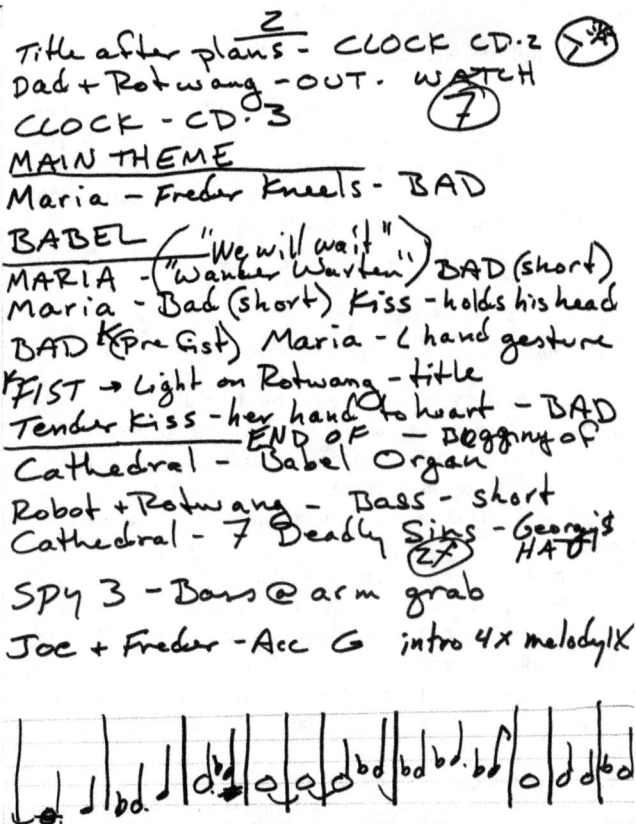

Figure 4.8 Excerpt from Terry Donahue's part from Alloy Orchestra's *Metropolis* score. Used by permission.

Donahue's score contains structural landmarks (BABEL), picture notes ("Maria hand gesture"), and musical reminders ("intro 4x melody 1x"). Additionally, Donahue sketched in some notation at the bottom of the page. Note the missing clef and time signature; these are not necessary since it is just a memory aid.

There are benefits to a word score: you can cover a lot of screen time in just one page, writing down only what's important or needs reminding. It has simplicity and efficiency.

There are drawbacks to a word score: it tends to be understandable only to whoever wrote it, or would require explanation to a substitute player. It is not complete documentation: revisiting it, say, ten years later, even its author might not remember what was intended.

Exercises or thought experiments

Find a short silent film or an excerpt from a feature-length silent film and write out a word score. What needs to be specified? Would you include any notation? Can you write a word score that is understandable by other players, as well as yourself? What makes the score more transparent or transportable? What makes it opaque?

Themes and cue book

The *themes and cue book* system, developed by the author, combines *two* elements: a *theme sheet* and a *cue book*. This system may require *two* music stands per player. Theme sheet(s) are open on one stand – to be read, or as an aide-mémoire given sufficient rehearsal – while a second stand holds the lengthier cue book, coil bound so pages can be easily turned and lay flat during performance.

The theme sheet comprises a page or pages that present all major themes, notated in some fashion or other, either in *short score*, lead sheets, or as individual parts (see Figure 4.9). A theme sheet can be provided in appropriate keys for transposing instruments, like clarinet or trumpet; it can be prepared in the appropriate clef for instruments like viola. In my experience, two to four pages of themes seems to be the sweet spot for most silent feature films.

The theme sheet in Figure 4.9 uses a variety of means to convey information and conserve space. The "Governor Theme" is shown as a chord progression, with a particular voicing presented in the first bars. You may infer that this theme is intended for low instruments; the chromatic descending bassline is a distinct musical feature. High instruments can accompany if desired by

Communicate your score 99

Figure 4.9 Excerpt from *The Mark of Zorro* theme sheets by Jack Curtis Dubowsky © 2017 De Stijl Music. These themes can be heard on the Jack Curtis Dubowsky Ensemble album, *Zorro* (2017).

following the chord chart. The [FR] or *fragment* version is a shorter iteration of the theme that can be cycled as a vamp.

A *short score* facilitates swapping parts or *voices* within an arrangement. "Troopers Theme" section [A] shows two independent voices which could be swapped; [B] shows only one melody, saving space on the page. In both sections, chords and bass are specified in the chart. "Pulidos Theme" section [A] is presented as a lead sheet; section [B] notates two independent outer voices, treble and bass, which are unlikely to be swapped.

You may notice omission of tempos. You *can* have tempos in a theme sheet; this is often a wise idea. In this case, as you might imagine, tempos are given by the conductor and/or are given *in the cue book*, so themes can adapt to different circumstances in the film. The book can restructure the music, so a theme might start on [B] rather than [A], or it might follow a unique *map*, or pattern of repetitions. Cues might end halfway through a theme; these unique timings can be handled by the conductor or added to the cue book.

Some of these themes could be memorized; even so, having theme sheets open during rehearsal or performance is practical and reassuring. Theme sheets work in conjunction with a *cue book*, which details the organizational structure of the whole score.

The *cue book* lists screen cues sequentially (see Figure 4.10). Every detail that needs attention can be listed, with time indices to facilitate rehearsal if desired. This provides written documentation of the whole film, scene-by-scene, shot-by-shot, or in any combination thereof, as needed. The cue book may be many pages long, depending on the level of detail.

The very process of preparing a cue book is helpful, not just for live performance, but for *spotting* and composition as well (as discussed in Chapter 2). The cue book lays out the film in a linear fashion, allowing you to see several minutes at once, including major topography (scenes), structural points, cards, and minor details ("They stop, SHAKE HANDS").

Begin preparing the cue book with the CUES column on the left. Then, you can use empty instrument lanes to sketch where themes start and stop, what will bridge scenes, and what will hit important action moments. As you continue to score the film, you see how instruments trade off, where *tuttis* are, how to make things dovetail or overlap, and how to keep things interesting musically and dramatically.

Each player has a column in the cue book. In the example shown, there are six players; the violinist doubles on viola, and the clarinetist doubles on bass clarinet. In each column are instructions for their own individual part. Box notation or instructions fit inside the column; boxes (or arrows) indicate durations.

Instructions can refer to a theme by name: "Illness" or "Happy Times," for instance.[14] (The music for those themes is on a theme sheet, so it is not necessary for it to appear in the cue book!) Some players might play a theme, while others simultaneously improvise characters ("MM Hutter," "MM Bulwer," MM being short for mickey-mouse), or create environmental effects or textures ("staccato soup"). This leads to greater depth and breadth in the score.

A map has been penciled in for the "Happy Times" theme: careful ordering of four sections, [1], [2], [3], and [4], and their repeats. The decision to place the theme here came *first*, and the precise calculation of the map for best effect worked out later.[15] Such a map can be written into the book or can be indicated by a conductor (holding up fingers), or both. Arrows indicate where flute, violin, and bass join the keyboard playing [1], approximately at the long

Communicate your score 101

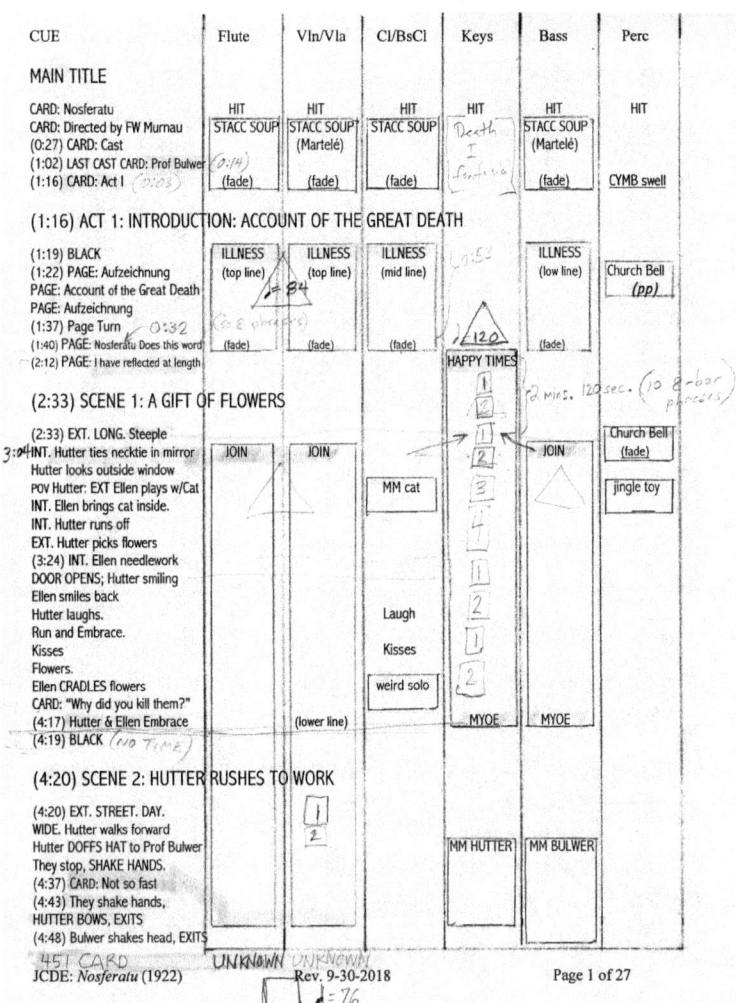

Figure 4.10 Excerpt from *Nosferatu* cue book by Jack Curtis Dubowsky © 2018 De Stijl Music.

shot of the steeple (2:33). Keys and bass end at the black before "SCENE 2," leaving flute and violin to carry on with a duet rendition of [1] and [2].

Notice that "Death [I] fantasia" has been *added* to the book in the keyboard part, penciled in at "CARD: Directed by." The cue book system makes

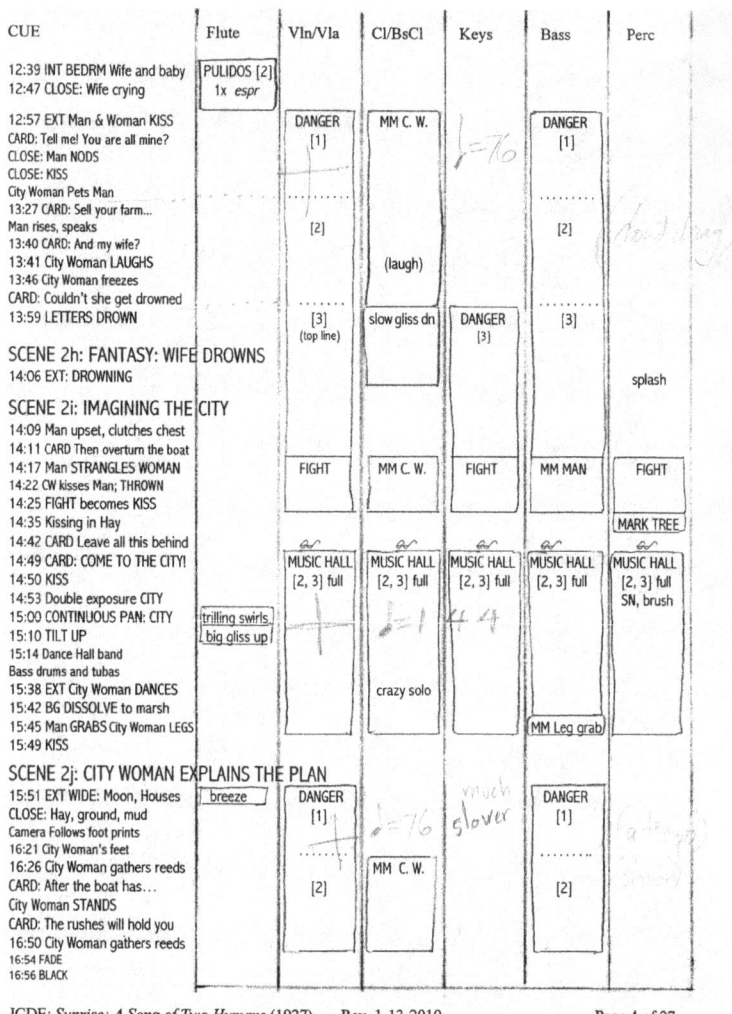

Figure 4.11 Excerpt from *Sunrise* cue book by Jack Curtis Dubowsky © 2019 De Stijl Music.

it relatively easy to add (or cut) things, whether in rehearsal or after much consideration (compared to rewriting a fully notated score).

Figure 4.11 shows an excerpt from another cue book, *Sunrise: A Song of Two Humans*. In this book, theme sections like "Danger" [1], [2], [3] are already figured out; dotted horizontal lines approximate where section changes occur. "Top line" in [3] violin specifies a part (or voice) within a theme notated in short score (or in multiple voices).

There are places where players pay attention to different things. When "Man strangles woman" (14:17), three players track the fight while one player mickey-mouses the man, another the woman. During the "Music Hall" *tutti*, five players play the theme while the flute tracks camera movement ("pan," "tilt up"), and the clarinet spins off into a "crazy solo" to hit the City Woman dancing (15:38). The bass spins off to mickey-mouse a "leg grab."

During Scene 2j, the flute plays an environmental effect ("breeze") against the violin and bass; the texture is thin here, so adding this flute effect works nicely, making the score richer.

At the very bottom of the page, care was taken to make an easy page turn. This is a concern with cue books, although you may notice that keys and bass could turn the page ahead of time. Sometimes, you may elect to *not* fill an entire page, if it will help a page turn. You may notice places where players can turn the page ahead of time, or where players can pencil in at the bottom what is coming next (see Figure 4.10). (Sometimes players can turn the page after the fact if needed.)

The themes and cue book system works best with a limited number of players, up to about eight at most, unless they are doubled on a part. Benefits include ease of rehearsals, accommodation of both structured improvisation *and* notated themes, independence of parts, and unique performances. A conductor (who may be one of the players) coordinates entrances and exits, especially of notated themes that are played together. A conductor may need to signal which section of a theme is coming up, by holding up a finger(s); for this reason, it is best not to exceed five sections per theme.

There are a few drawbacks to this system. Players must focus their attention on *four* places: (1) watching the screen, (2) watching the conductor, (3) following the cue book, and (4) consulting theme sheets as necessary. With practice, this becomes easier: players learn to watch the screen when improvising but turn their attention toward the conductor when a group entrance is approaching.

This system tends to encourage thematic writing that is succinct and modular; this might not be everyone's cup of tea. But succinct and modular writing often benefits film scoring; being able to shift or end a theme quickly helps fit themes to tight onscreen timings more easily.

Exercises or thought experiments

Find a short silent film or an excerpt from a feature-length silent film.

1. Make a cue book, without any instrument lanes yet, just writing down all the cues, cards, and significant moments that may inform

the score. See how much detail you can get in. See how you can best abbreviate cues and cards. Try using indications such as Int. and Ext. for interior and exterior. Try notating camera angles if needed: "2 shot," "wide," "long," "close," and so on.
2. Using three lanes, see what kind of structure you can concoct. You can plan the themes topographically, but do not compose them at this point. Consider what the themes would be composed for: certain characters? Certain places? Certain ideas?
3. Using five lanes, see what kind of structure you can make.
4. Knowing now what themes you need or want, go and compose them. How well does it all fit together? Could you also write the themes in advance, and then make the cue book?

Conductor hand symbols

A bandleader, composer, or conductor may develop their own vocabulary of hand signals and instruct an ensemble on their interpretation. These signals can be tailored to a particular film and for any musical effect desired. Once the ensemble knows the signals, the conductor can compose a score in advance or improvise one on the fly. The players may not need any sheet music if the signals can be memorized.

This technique comes out of compositional games by John Zorn (like *Cobra*)[16] and the *conduction* techniques of Butch Morris (1947–2013). Figure 4.12 shows how Butch Morris would indicate an arpeggio – this does not, on its own, specify pitches; these might be indicated separately (or not at all), and tempo might be suggested by the speed of the gesture.

Benefits to using hand symbols, or some form of conduction, include minimal rehearsal time, once the vocabulary of signals is learned. If signals are clear and unambiguous, any player can learn them; they can be reused for different films. Players need to watch the conductor to know when and what to play, rather than necessarily having to see the screen.

Another benefit is unique performances – no two shows will sound alike, given the vast amount of variance in response to signals. (This can be seen as a drawback, depending on your intentions.) This approach allows for players' creativity and input: you want an arpeggio? Fine. I will play an arpeggio that I like and think will work here.

There are drawbacks to this approach. Not all players may be comfortable or interested in this approach; some (who are inexperienced with improvisation or forget signals) may choke or lag under duress. Audiences may miss hearing clear, consistent, memorable, melodic themes they associate with film music. Performances may be chaotic and at times unpredictable, and

Communicate your score 105

Figure 4.12 Butch Morris arpeggio indication: "Arpeggio. When the directive is given, followed by a down beat, the instrumentalist elaborates and embellishes whatever she/he is doing through arpeggiation." Laurence D. "Butch" Morris. *The Art of Conduction – A Conduction Workbook*, Daniela Veronesi Ed. (New York: Karma). ©2017 Lawrence Butch Morris Legacy Project. Used by permission.

may not always succeed in closely tracking the film. Timing may suffer if the conductor doesn't know the film adequately or if the ensemble responds unevenly.

Conductor hand symbols can be combined with other methods. Many conductor gestures are already standardized, such as crescendos, diminuendos, beat patterns, and regulating tempo. A conductor may make a sad face or a happy face to emphasize how a scene or moment should be played. Techniques can be combined; a composer might write a "main theme" and assign a hand signal to indicate that theme should be played as composed.

> **Exercises or thought experiments**
>
> Find a silent short or feature film excerpt.
>
> 1. What musical gestures would you have a group of players do to accompany the film? What musical gestures would be especially effective or useful? Consider sounds which are abstract, atonal, not centered around pitch, but are still expressive.
> 2. Create some hand gestures for these ideas.
> 2. Find some players and try this out. How well did it work? What gestures were memorable? What gestures were confusing or complicated? How well did people follow your gestures?

Combinations

These techniques and systems can be combined. Overtures or closing music might be fully notated, while other sections are improvised using a word score or other notational method.

Nosferatu, as supplied on 35mm film, begins with an "Overture" card – no screen action, simply that card, holding for 1:25. My ensemble adopted sheet music for that overture; we then hit the following card "Nosferatu" all together, and move right into the cue book (see Figure 4.10).

A conductor using a vocabulary of hand gestures can have a unique signal (or signals) to play a particular theme (or themes) which can be notated or learned in advance. This combines conduction with pre-composed material, allowing a large ensemble to entirely pivot from abstract interpretation to a precise tune. This conductor could also use such a signal to have *some players* play the notated theme, while others overlap it with something else.

You might have a short score that incorporates box notation or graphic notation, or that explodes into multiple staves when greater detail is necessary. Text instructions can be added to any score, to help clarify a desired effect if parts are notated or incorporate extended techniques.

You might have a situation where different players have their own extracted, personalized parts, but one may have a word score, and another may have a notated score, or something else. In *Sunrise*, we had an organ solo in the cathedral (ca. 00:41:15), for which the keyboardist and bassist alone had notated parts. No one else was playing; others followed along in the cue book, while the bassist and keyboardist took a detour on one page of sheet music.

You may imagine other combinations that suit your goals and intentions. Switching between systems can be disorienting, but it can work well. It's wise to choose *in advance* notation types and means of communicating your score, as this will speed up its preparation. Available forces, rehearsal time, and the film itself may inform these decisions. If you can only afford one "run through" with your group, notation will need to be straightforward, whatever system you adopt.

Knowing your players' strengths and limitations helps ascertain the best approach. Some players may be thrown off by complex notation. Other players may be thrown by a *lack* of clear notation. In the best of all possible worlds, you will have a system that fits your music and time enough to rehearse it with your players.

Exercises or thought experiments

Try combining some of these systems on your own, or create new systems.
What worked well? What did not?

Conducting techniques and issues

Sight lines and visibility

As discussed in Chapter 3, in the section on choice of ensemble, you may want a conductor to help communicate your score, especially in a large group, or where players need help with cues, entrances, and tempos.

Conductor and players need to see each other. The conductor needs to see the film. If the score is *fully notated*, or if all players completely follow *conduction* or similar guides, players may need only to see the *conductor*. This scenario facilitates seating arrangements, and lets players face the audience, with the conductor facing the screen *and* the players.

While this arrangement may be traditional and familiar to concertgoers (and rather hierarchical, we may note), there are other ways to perform a live score, as this book discusses. Depending on techniques used, like *mickey-mousing* or *improvisation*, the screen may need to be visible to *players* as well. Everyone may need to see the screen at some point. Given limited space in an orchestra pit or cinema, some creative seating or screen monitoring solutions may be considered. Figure 4.13 shows a setup where *players face the screen*; the conductor uses a tablet to see the screen, as discussed further below.

A live score environment can be a two-way street. It's not simply a matter of players following a conductor. The conductor should be able to read the players as well. Players may give information to the conductor: they may

108 *Communicate your score*

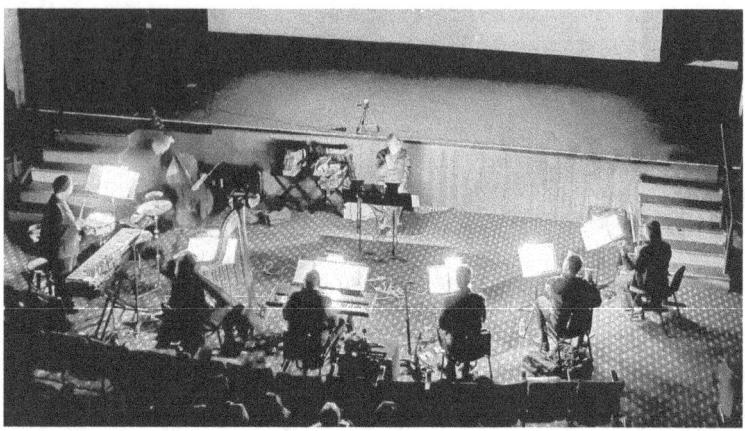

Figure 4.13 Jack Curtis Dubowsky Ensemble players face the screen; conductor has a tablet to see film. Photo by Karen Axelton-Dibble.

indicate they need a cue; they may look at the screen to show they know their cue from the screen; they may indicate they are lost, they are having trouble hearing another player, or they are annoyed that another player is stomping all over their part (for example, if players are mickey-mousing a scene together). This book encourages collaboration and improvisation in performance. The conductor is not the apex of a hierarchy, but rather a bus driver, keeping everyone together, not hanging out the windows. The conductor knows the road they are traveling, including its hazards.

The conductor should *know the film* really well, to follow inferior image quality or tricky sightlines. Ideally, the conductor has the film memorized, and just needs to orient themselves temporally within the film. Players who need to play onscreen action and mickey-mouse should be given preferential view of the screen.

In cases where it is technically feasible, the conductor may have their own video feed from the projection booth. Figure 4.14 shows the conductor's video feed from *Sunrise: A Song of Two Humans* score for orchestra and chorus by Jeff Beal. Note the *condensed score* at the bottom, enlarged rehearsal mark [I2], cue name [6. The Boat Ride], and bar and beat numbers [600|4]. The vertical *streamer* on the right, shown mid-travel across the screen, indicates an upcoming rehearsal mark and sync point, [K2]. (Additionally, a thin vertical line moves through the condensed score, likely not visible on this printed page.)

This video feed (Figure 4.14) allows a conductor to achieve precise synchronization; the orchestra and chorus follow the conductor without having

Figure 4.14 Sunrise: A Song of Two Humans score for orchestra and chorus by Jeff Beal, conductor video feed. ©2019 St. Rose Music Publishing Co. Inc. and Associated Music Publishers, Inc. Used by permission.

to see the screen. The composer can have a highly accurate reproduction of their intention. This method imposes technical and budgetary demands on the preparation and production of the score.

While, in theory, giving the conductor a dedicated video feed sounds reasonable, in practice it is often difficult: ordinary movie theaters are typically not set up to do this and have no provision for splitting off and running a video line that would need to be hundreds of feet in length. In cases where theaters are projecting actual 35mm film, it is virtually impossible: there simply is no video feed at all, just light from the projector. A practical solution in these cases is to have the conductor use a tablet to see the screen behind them.

Large-screen tablets are now commonly used to read sheet music, and there are many options available for mounting tablets to microphone stands or music stands. The tablet is put in a "selfie" camera mode, locked on, and positioned so the conductor sees the screen behind themselves. This can be done with a mobile phone, although having a larger tablet screen makes it easier. The tablet in Figure 4.15 is attached to a microphone stand using a commercially available mount. It can be angled to show the screen behind the conductor. The tablet's camera exposure setting should be locked so the image remains clear and in focus. A power cable, while perhaps unnecessary, ensures the tablet remains charged under unforeseen circumstances.

One issue with a tablet as rearview mirror is that the image will be *flipped*: things on the left will appear on the right, and text on intertitle cards will be *backwards*. All the more reason the conductor must know the film exceedingly well and rehearse with the mirrored image.

110 Communicate your score

Figure 4.15 Conductor and author Jack Curtis Dubowsky facing ensemble with tablet to see screen. Photo by Scott Heustis.

Clarity

With players in the dark, distracted by the film, audience, sheet music, and perhaps a cue book, it helps for the conductor to be as clear and large as possible. This is not an environment where players look for subtle gestures. They are trying their best to keep it together, and clarity is essential.

Beat patterns should be clear, consistent, and visible. Like a bus driver, the conductor should know the hazards of the road and know when a turn is coming up. Cues for particular players should be comfortably prepared – even if this is just eye contact – and not thrown out in a last-second panic. Tempos should be established clearly and confidently.

Cueing entrances and exits

How entrances and exits are conducted should be established during rehearsal and kept consistent. Using standard beat patterns will help musicians, rather than "pulling taffy" or having vague baton technique. Proper conducting techniques – those commonly and readily understood by musicians – can be learned in a group class or individual lessons, and are documented in many conducting textbooks.[17]

A single player's entrance may be confirmed with just a nod or a welcoming hand, opened palm-up. A moment of mutual recognition doesn't require any more than that. Avoid micromanaging soloists, especially those handling mickey-mousing, as it can be distracting. An exception might be a situation where a soloist needs help keeping time, so the score stays on track.

Groups of players and *tuttis* require attention, so players enter *together* and *in time*. How you conduct these entrances depends upon tempo, meter, and time available before their entrance or onscreen *sync point*. Does the conductor give just an upbeat, two beats, a whole measure? The conductor should work out group entrances in advance, practicing the film on their own. These entrances can be adjusted or refined in rehearsal, but ought to be solid and predictable by performance time.

Helping balances

An important role of the conductor is to help balances in an impartial way, so that some players don't overwhelm others, and proper balances are achieved musically and for dramatic effect.

Early rehearsals are best left for getting through the whole film and fine-tuning arrangements. Balances can be addressed in subsequent rehearsals. Balances tend to work themselves out over time: once players know what is going on and start listening to each other, they tend to balance themselves without much adjustment. Listening to others is a skill, and playing live scores helps players listen to each other.

While balances can be worked on in rehearsal, once you get to a performance venue with different acoustics, it can be a different matter. Having a few minutes to sound check and play through *tuttis* or passages with varying dynamics and instrumentation is a necessity. Players can hear the acoustics and rebalance; the conductor can run into the auditorium, listen, and give impartial notes on how to compensate for the acoustic qualities of the space.

Another issue is balancing mickey-mousing against musical themes that play simultaneously. Coaching mickey-mousing is discussed above in the improvisation section. A conductor may manage how subtle or blatant mickey-mousing is as a matter of balance and register.

Tempos and dynamics

The conductor bears responsibility for having the ensemble proceed at the correct tempo, essential for synchronization in live performance. Different players, with differing amounts of orchestra or musical theater pit experience, may respond differently to a conductor: some players may feel sluggish, some highly responsive. Rehearsals help a score settle where it needs to be, to hit all the marks in the right place. Ideally, a conductor will be confident, patient with players, and own up to their own mistakes, which do happen.

A good conductor helps the score become more musical, shepherding nuances of speed and dynamics: *accelerandi, ritardandi, rallentandi, allargandi, stringendi, crescendi,* and *dimenuendi.* The conductor can help provide overall perspective to a score, shaping it so it ebbs and flows, builds and subsides, and works to support the picture and remain musical at the same time.

Individual players may focus on their own parts and shining moments, while the conductor can ascertain what the score needs as a *whole*. Sometimes, this justifies having a conductor for a smaller ensemble that might *not* need one for, say, classical chamber music. Live scores can be complex and detailed. A conductor looks out for everyone's entrances, exits, timings, tempos, and dynamics. While conductors should avoid micromanaging players, they can be a source of support and confirmation.

Exercises or thought experiments

One standard conducting exercise helpful for silent film scores is to learn and memorize tempos. Can you conduct an accurate qu=120 on demand? How about qu=88, or qu=144? Using a metronome, learn and conduct a variety of tempos, in different meters too. (Use standard metronome markings; they appear frequently in published sheet music, and are familiar to the widest variety of players.) Sometimes it helps to think of a particular recording of a piece of music, and recall that in your mind, to recall a particular tempo.

Once you have learned tempos, you can check them against a metronome. Try checking them under different circumstances: can you reproduce an accurate tempo whether you are tired, sleepy, excited, on an empty stomach, or after having a cup of coffee?

Equipment

To effectively communicate your score to an audience, you depend on having proper equipment at the show. It is advisable to have a *checklist* of gear needed for the performance. This can include music stands, stand lights, power strips, power cables, instrument stands, and amplifiers. It can also include promotional items, like merch, and notes for introducing the film. Your needs will vary, of course, but you want to know that everything will be there.

> **Exercises or thought experiments**
>
> Given the players and gear at your disposal, write out an equipment list for yourself, or for the group as a whole. What do you need to bring? What would cause problems if lost or forgotten? Are there any items for which you would bring extras or a backup?

A conclusion

Composing for silent film offers creative opportunities for unconventional, avant-garde music *and* the chance to make something genuinely appreciated by a large audience. This overlap of creativity and appreciation is something very precious to musicians.

Here's some context. While working in Hollywood "show business" – with its petty demands, pedestrian tastes, and "sausage making" mentality – I struggled to get "new music" ensembles to program a five-minute piece to an audience of 40 folding chairs.[18]

At the same time, I built under my own name a group that could sell out a historic theater with hundreds and sometimes thousands of seats. Especially towards the beginning, these scores could be pretty corny at times, which is how I developed my distaste for film funning and other banal techniques.

The more I watched and rehearsed silent films, the more I noticed. It took me repeated viewings to realize that *mirrors* are a central theme in *Dr. Jekyll and Mr. Hyde*, because everyone needs to see themselves to know how far they have fallen.[19] It took repeated viewings to realize how portrayals of Indigenous people permeate *The Mark of Zorro*.[20] It took repeated viewings to realize *why* The Wife carries a scarf throughout most of *Sunrise*.[21]

In grasping the depth and subtlety of silent film, I slowly put my finger on what was *missing* from others' live score performances: attention to this level of detail. If I could faithfully bring out all these details for a spectator who was watching a film for the first (or even the tenth) time, it would be a whole new magnificent experience. And indeed, after seeing our live scores, many silent film fans told us they had picked up on things they had *never noticed before*.

You can do this too. Regardless of your level of training, whether you have an orchestra or a kazoo, there is music to be made, audiences to entertain. Live scores are live performance, where mistakes can be made and accidents occur. You have a chance to make music that is not a grab bag of current "film music" clichés, but something that highlights your own unique voice.

Much contemporary concert music is reflexively touted as "experimental." In live scores, you can make *actual* experiments: you can try things in different ways. You can change things up. You can try repeating an experiment and

114 Communicate your score

see if you get the same reaction from a different audience. You can work on a score as much as you like, refining it as you better know the film and show your work to different audiences. There is no deadline, no final version. The score becomes, ultimately, an abstraction. It exists as a set of instructions you give to your players, their interpretation of it, and an idealized version that can never be fully notated. It doesn't need to be performed exactly the same way twice; people will come back to see it again and again. This keeps silent film alive and vibrant for today and tomorrow.

Notes

1. Dubowsky, Jack Curtis. (2021). *Easy Listening and Film Scoring 1948–78*. (New York: Routledge).
2. Eisler, Hanns. (1941). "Film Music–work in progress" in *Historical Journal of Film, Radio and Television*, Vol. 18, No. 4, 1998. p. 591.
3. See Dubowsky, Jack Curtis. (2016). *Intersecting Film, Music, and Queerness*. (Basingstoke: Palgrave). pp. 31–5.
4. Eisler, Hanns. (1941). "Film Music–work in progress" in *Historical Journal of Film, Radio and Television*, Vol. 18, No. 4, 1998. p. 592.
5. Audiovisual technician and historian Stephen Handzo attributes the term "mickey-mousing" to producer David O. Selznick (1902–65) describing a score by Max Steiner that followed action with cartoon-like accuracy. Handzo, Stephen. (1985). "Appendix: A Narrative Glossary of Film Sound Techniques" in *Film Found: Theory and Practice*. Edited by E. Weis and G. Belton, G. pp. 409–10. (New York: Columbia University Press).
6. Bar charts (or bar sheets) are discussed in Tietyen, David. (1990). *The Musical World of Walt Disney*. pp. 13–14. (Milwaukee, WI: Hal Leonard); Goldmark, Daniel. (2005). *Tunes for 'Toons: Music and the Hollywood Cartoon*. p. 20. (Berkeley, CA: University of California Press); and Levitan, Eli L. (1962). *Animation Art in the Commercial Film*. pp. 62, 185. (New York: Reinhold).
7. Responsiveness to onscreen action in film is discussed in Chapter 2, "Musical Cachet in *The Living End* and the New Queer Cinema" in Dubowsky, Jack Curtis. (2016). *Intersecting Film, Music, and Queerness*. (Basingstoke:Palgrave).
8. For further discussion of the use of mood music or easy listening music in mid-century film scores, see Dubowsky, Jack Curtis. (2021). *Easy Listening and Film Scoring 1948–78*. (New York, NY:Routledge).
9. London, Kurt. Translated by Eric S. Bensinger. (1936). *Film Music: A Summary of the Characteristic Features of Its History, Aesthetics, Technique; and Possible Developments*. (London: Faber & Faber Ltd.). p. 41. (Emphasis in original; written in 1933 according to the dust jacket.)
10. Erdmann, Hans, Becce, Giuseppe, and Brav, Ludwig. (1927). *Allgemeines Handbuch der Film- Musik*. (Berlin-Lichterfelde, Leipzig: Schlesinger). (2020 reprint: Berlin: Ries & Erler).
11. Rapée, Ernö. (1924). *Motion Picture Moods for Pianists and Organists*. (New York: G. Schirmer, Inc.).
12. Bailey, Derek. (1992). *Improvisation: Its Nature and Practice in Music*. (Boston, MA: Da Capo Press). pp. xi–xii.
13. Donahue, Terry. (2021). Email to author. July 6.
14. The indication "JOIN" means to join the keyboard already playing the theme. "MYOE" means "make your own exit," presumably at the end of a phrase, to be ready

for the approaching mickey-mousing. In practice, it helps to have a conductor assist these entrances and exits. You can invent your own abbreviations for instructions.
15 You can see some penciled calculations: at qu=120, ten 8-bar phrases will be 120 seconds, or two minutes. This covers the keyboard's section from (2:12) "I have reflected" to (4:17) "Embrace."
16 A four-page PDF of a set of rules to John Zorn's unpublished *Cobra* (1984) can be found online on various websites. As of this writing, it can be found at https://hermes.neocities.org/zorn-cobra-score.pdf and at https://web.archive.org/web/20130128204544/http://www.4-33.com/scores/cobra/cobra-notes.html (accessed June 28, 2023).
17 There are many basic, practical conducting textbooks. Two examples are: Bailey, Wayne. (2009). *Conducting: The Art of Communication*. (New York: Oxford University Press); and Phillips, Kenneth H. (1997). *Basic Techniques of Conducting*. (New York: Oxford University Press).
18 I'm putting "scare quotes" around these common expressions. The particular "show business" I mean here is the world of studio and network film and television. "How the sausage is made" is a common expression for the below-the-line work in film and television, whose processes are standardized and formulaic. "New music" is a genre of contemporary concert music – widely discussed by authors including Alex Ross, Will Robin, Paul Griffiths, and others – that functions largely to advance academic careers in coordination with a highly networked and competitive arts industrial complex.
19 The tip off for this, for me, was the mirror in the opium den. *Wait, why would there even be a mirror in an opium den?* *lightbulb*
20 It should be noted that *The Mark of Zorro* is also a classic "white savior" story, which became a common Hollywood movie trope. Still, and notably for the time period, the consistently positive Indigenous portrayals are an attempt to give the film greater depth and realism.
21 When the scarf is found floating in the water (ca. 01:24:20), the audience should infer that the Wife has drowned.

Bibliography

Altman, Rick. (2004). *Silent Film Sound* (New York: Columbia University Press).
Bailey, Derek. (1992). *Improvisation: Its Nature and Practice in Music* (Boston, MA: Da Capo Press).
Bailey, Wayne. (2009). *Conducting: The Art of Communication* (New York: Oxford University Press).
Dubowsky, Jack Curtis. (2016). *Intersecting Film, Music, and Queerness* (Basingstoke: Palgrave).
Dubowsky, Jack Curtis. (2021). *Easy Listening and Film Scoring 1948–78* (New York: Routledge).
Eisler, Hanns. (1941). "Film Music–work in progress." *Historical Journal of Film, Radio and Television*, Vol. 18, No. 4, 1998.
Erdmann, Hans, Becce, Giuseppe, and Brav, Ludwig. (1927). *Allgemeines Handbuch der Film-Musik* (Berlin-Lichterfelde, Leipzig: Schlesinger) (2020 reprint: Berlin: Ries & Erler).
Goldmark, Daniel. (2005). *Tunes for 'Toons: Music and the Hollywood Cartoon* (Berkeley, CA: University of California Press), p. 20.
Handzo, Stephen. (1985). "Appendix: A Narrative Glossary of Film Sound Techniques." In *Film Found: Theory and Practice*. Edited by E. Weis and G. Belton (New York: Columbia University Press), pp. 409–10.

Levitan, Eli L. (1962). *Animation Art in the Commercial Film* (New York: Reinhold), pp. 62, 185.

London, Kurt. (1936). *Film Music: A Summary of the Characteristic Features of Its History, Aesthetics, Technique; and Possible Developments.* Translated by Eric S. Bensinger (London: Faber & Faber Ltd.).

Phillips, Kenneth H. (1997). *Basic Techniques of Conducting* (New York: Oxford University Press).

Rapée, Ernö. (1924). *Motion Picture Moods for Pianists and Organists* (New York: G. Schirmer, Inc.).

Roads, Curtis. (1996). *The Computer Music Tutorial* (Cambridge, MA: The MIT Press).

Roads, Curtis. (2023). *The Computer Music Tutorial*, Second Edition (Cambridge, MA: The MIT Press).

Shockley, Alan. (2018). *The Contemporary Piano: A Performer and Composer's Guide to Techniques and Resources* (New York: Rowman & Littlefield).

Tietyen, David. (1990). *The Musical World of Walt Disney* (Milwaukee, WI: Hal Leonard), pp. 13–14.

Zorn, John. (1984). *Cobra* (New York: Unpublished manuscript).

For Product Safety Concerns and Information please contact our EU representative GPSR@taylorandfrancis.com
Taylor & Francis Verlag GmbH, Kaufingerstraße 24, 80331 München, Germany

www.ingramcontent.com/pod-product-compliance
Lightning Source LLC
Chambersburg PA
CBHW051752230426
43670CB00012B/2255

Bibliography (for further reference see)

Clason, W. E. (1956). *Elsevier's Dictionary of Cinema Sound and Music* (New York: Elsevier Publishing Company).

Miller, Tony and George, Patricia. (1977). *"Cut! Print!": The Language and Structure of Filmmaking* (Van Nuys: F.I.W. Press).

Glossary 121

sound effects general term referring to sounds made to enhance a motion picture. Can be musical or extra-musical, diegetic or non-diegetic.
spoiler surprise (if revealed would spoil the movie for an uninitiated viewer).
spotting making decisions where music will go and what it will do.
spotting notes documentation from a spotting meeting.
story an underlying framework that supports plot, narrative, and what happens.
streamer in film music conducting, a vertical line traveling across the screen to indicate an upcoming sync point.
subplot narrative element within a greater whole; story within a story; a character's own story within a larger context. Subplots add depth, complexity, motivation, and rationale to a dramatic work.
subtitles text, often translation of dialogue, that is burned into the lower third of a motion picture frame.
suspension of disbelief in drama, the desirable situation where an audience understands and accepts what transpires on stage or on screen. Its foundation is an imaginary world that obeys its own established logic.
sync point place where picture and sound synchronize or match perfectly; adjustments might be made to the head or tail end of a section, but the sync point always needs to be spot on.
talkies nickname for sound film, especially with spoken dialogue.
technobabble invented, frequently nonsensical pseudoscientific jargon created for science fiction films and similar dramatic situations.
tentpole scenes critical sequences, often major dramatic turning points.
themes (drama) recurring arguments, messages, and ideas explored in a work.
themes (music) melodies, motives, or recognizable musical gestures that recur in a larger work; these can be tied to characters, ideas, places, events, and so on.
trope (film) a common (or overused) device, situation, or narrative idea.
trope (music) a common (or overused) device, convention, or technique.
tutti all instruments playing.
voice (music) in polyphony, an individual line; three-part harmony typically has a high voice, a low voice, and an inner voice.
visual effects a broad, categorical term for specially created imagery; sometimes called special effects.
wide shot camera shot from a distance that shows a complete view of a person, object, location, or situation and its surroundings.
worldbuilding in drama and film, the creation of fictional environments with their own logic, rules, imagery, sounds, and situations, especially in science fiction and fantasy.

period (music theory) two or more phrases that combine to make a longer melody.

photoplay motion picture scenario; portmanteau dating from the Nickelodeon era, in particular 1910–15, combining photography and play, often used synonymously with motion picture, emphasizing the idea of a play in pictures.

pick-up (film) an added shoot, to add missing details or fix issues with scenes shot earlier.

pitch set (music) group of selected pitches; these do not need to belong to any scale or mode.

plot the organization of story into structural elements such as acts, scenes, and order of exposition.

point of view (camera) a shot filmed from how a particular character would see it.

prelap music or sound that precedes and leads us into a following scene or location. (Can be used as a noun or verb.)

prepared piano in contemporary music, a piano that has been modified to make unusual sounds, often by inserting objects in its strings.

reaction shot a shot of a character(s) reacting to something. Can provide information about what happened, its gravity or humor; gives the film editor footage to cut to avoid a static shot. Sometimes relied upon to amplify action, for example, if a visual effect is not convincing, the reaction indicates how the director would like it perceived.

reel container for film wound around a spool and protected by flanges. A reel is loaded into a projector to be projected.

register (musical) a frequency range, high or low, where an instrument or voice lives comfortably.

restorations films preserved, repaired, and otherwise readied for renewed viewing. Processes involved are time consuming and expensive; restorations are subject to copyright for the work done, even if the underlying dramatic work (story, characters, imagery) is public domain.

reveal the onscreen moment an audience sees or learns something.

scherzo a fast piece of music.

screen time the total amount of time a character or object appears onscreen in a film.

sequence (film) a section with a logical thread; can be a group of continuous scenes. Often isolated for concentrated work (scoring, editing, refining).

sequence (music) a brief musical phrase or motive that repeats and alters through modulation or changes in underlying chords or harmony.

sight lines what people can see in the positioning of an ensemble for film; the matrix of visibility in arranging a group.

sneak a sound or musical gesture for a character sneaking.

intertitles   text, often dialogue or exposition, that occurs on a card within a silent film.
jump cut   in film editing, a picture cut within a shot that skips across time or missing footage, either accidentally or intentionally for a desired effect.
jump scare   especially in contemporary horror film, a scare that is affected or amplified by a sudden picture cut or loud sound.
looping (music)   music created or extended through the use of audio loops, either digitally or through tape, using hardware or software.
lower-third (film)   the lower third portion of the screen, typically in television, where text conventionally appears for subtitles or other information; this area is sometimes referred to as a Chyron after a character generator used to make them.
magazine   part of the motion picture camera that holds the film.
male gaze   the subjectivity of the camera eye that forces a heteronormative male viewpoint of spectatorship; the way a film is presented through a masculine lens, along with evocations of male desire and the centering of male heterosexuality and perspectives.
melodic contour   the shape of a melody, how it rises and falls in pitch, without specifying those exact pitches or modality.
mickey-mousing   musically imitating onscreen character action or dialogue.
mood music   music setting a prolonged mood, rather than following dramatic action.
Motion Picture Production Code   see Hays Code.
motivation   explanation of why characters behave a certain way, what motivates their actions.
muscle memory   means by which musical performance or physical activities are reproduced through repetitive action, rather than conscious intellectual recollection
narrative   the aspect of story that is told from a particular point of view.
nonlinear   a dramatic structure in which events are *not* revealed in chronological order.
non-narrative   a film, story, or dramatic work that avoids the order and point of view imposed by narration or narrative structure. These works are often abstract or require the spectator to superimpose their own perceptions onto the work.
ostinato   a repeating musical figure, often used as a motoric gesture or to spin a musical fabric of any length necessary.
outline (plot)   an overview or abbreviation of the plot and its sequential structures.
parallel action   scenes that happen at the same *time*, but not in the same location; the film *cuts between them*. (A film could have parallel action cutting between past and future events; this is less common.)

cue list   a list of musical pieces in a film, or a list of events in a film.
cue sheet   a list of musical pieces in a film. In the silent period, musical selections for an accompanist to play. In contemporary media scoring, detailed documentation of every cue in a film for performing rights organizations.
depth of field   in photography or cinematography, the range in focus, when objects are present near and far, as opposed to being blurry. In film, this is often used to direct our attention.
development (character)   the way a character grows and changes over time.
development (music)   manipulation, variation, and exploration of established musical material.
diegetic sound   sounds that are audible within the film world, that can be heard by characters onscreen.
dolly shot   motion picture photography taken from a dolly, a mobile platform attached to tracks on the ground.
double (music)   a musician who can play a number of instruments.
elevator pitch   summary of a movie in a few sentences to encourage its sale, investment, or a green light for production.
establish   in film, to make sure the audience knows about something.
establishing shot   typically a wide shot at the beginning of a scene, often an exterior, to indicate where the scene is taking place.
eye trace   Walter Murch term, the movement of the eye across the screen.
exposition   the way details of plot or narrative are revealed.
extras   ancillary actors, usually with no speaking lines, often entry level or amateur participants
film funning   accompanists' music that deliberately mocks a motion picture.
flashback   movement in the plotline that jumps back in time to show the past.
flashforward   movement in the plotline that jumps forward to show the future.
fragment (music)   a snippet of a longer theme; can be introduced, used, manipulated, or developed on its own.
generative music   music that generates itself through a set of established parameters.
Hays Code   Motion Picture Production Code, first proposed in 1927 and in effect from 1934 to 1968; censored or suppressed content that was considered morally or socially unacceptable.
intellectual property (IP)   any kind of creative work or invention that can be protected by copyright or trademark. Work that is both the product of creative, artistic, and intellectual labor and to which ownership can be affixed.

Glossary

archetype in literature and film, a character type or story readily and communally understood by an audience. The good man unjustly framed who has become an outlaw but has the moral high ground, for example.
backstory the story behind fictional characters, their motivation and history, whether presented onscreen or not.
blocking how actors are positioned and move relative to the camera.
bookends related scenes or images that start and end a film or sequence.
cards an area for text across the whole screen.
comping in music (especially jazz), a method of improvising a part over a given chord chart.
composite optical printing a technique using an optical printer and layers of film that makes dissolves, transitions, and various visual effects, by rephotographing the film frame by frame.
condensed score a score, in two to four staves, that condenses the parts in a larger full score.
conduction (music) a conducting and composition technique developed by Butch Morris whereby a vocabulary of gestures informs spontaneous improvisation and performance.
conforming adjusting music to match changes in the picture edit of a film.
continuity (film) the concern for keeping everything temporally continuous, so props don't mysteriously appear or disappear, clothing and hairstyles remain constant, and sequences of events remain logical (unless otherwise intended).
controlled acting acting approach advocated by Coquelin, Pennington, and others, in which the actor remains in control of their emotions, in order to better perform through practiced gestures.
coverage (film) film shot from a variety of angles and multiple takes, to allow the film editor to cut a scene that isn't just one static shot, or that is missing desired shots.
crane shot motion picture photography taken from a crane, enabling high views and dramatic camera motion.
cue (music) a piece of music in a film; can refer to the place in a film where a piece of music will go, delimited by its start and stop points.